The Inner Battlefield

Overcoming the Enemies

of the Mind and Soul

The Real War Is Within

Win it, and you win everything.

SHREE SHAMBAV

The Inner Battlefield –

Overcoming the Enemies of the Mind and Soul

Shree Shambav

Published by Shree Shambav, Tamil Nadu, India
Shree Shambav Ink & Imagination "Where Words Breathe and Imagination Soars"

First Edition, 2025

ISBN: 978-93-342-8347-1

Email: shreeshambav@gmail.com
Web: www.shambav.org

DEDICATION

"Isavasyam idam sarvam yat kim ca jagatyam jagat, tena tyaktena bhunjitha, ma gridhah kasyasvid dhanam"

To the Almighty,

the Divine Masters,

the family who listens,

and my parents who see –

your presence shapes the pages of my life's journey.

"Isavasyam idam sarvam yat kim ca jagatyam jagat"

Meaning: "God encompasses everything you perceive, see, or touch with your sense organs."

DISCLAIMER

The real war is within—win it, and you win everything.

In The Inner Battlefield, Shree Shambav extends an invitation to delve deep into the unseen terrain of the soul, where profound battles are fought against the forces of desire, anger, greed, attachment, pride, and jealousy. This book draws upon timeless spiritual wisdom and offers insights into transcending these internal adversaries to uncover lasting peace.

While this journey may inspire and guide, it is not a substitute for professional advice, nor does it claim to guarantee specific outcomes. Personal transformation is as unique as the individual undertaking it, requiring courage, discernment, and an unwavering commitment to self-awareness. The author and publisher emphasise that the insights shared within this book are tools to illuminate your path, not mandates for action.

By engaging with this material, you accept full responsibility for your journey, recognizing that every step—whether it brings clarity or challenge—is an integral part of your growth. This book does not offer shortcuts or absolutes but instead provides a compassionate framework to inspire reflection, encourage inquiry, and nurture personal evolution.

Take what resonates, honor your intuition, and embrace your capacity to transform. Remember, the ultimate guide to your inner battlefield lies within you—the quiet voice of truth, ever-present and ready to lead you toward freedom and fulfillment.

Note - If any part of the book, in any sequence, hurts the reader's sentiments, it would be just out of a sheer accident, not intentional

EPIGRAM

The Inner Battlefield

"Within the silence of the soul lies the fiercest battlefield; conquer the enemies within, and the world becomes yours to embrace."

– Shree Shambav

The Inner Battlefield

Overcoming the Enemies

of the Mind and Soul

Shree Shambav

Shree Shambav is a 30x best-selling author renowned for his transformative works in personal development and spiritual growth.

Dear Cherished Readers

Dear Cherished Readers,

As I embark on this new literary voyage, my heart swells with profound gratitude and an overwhelming sense of connection. With deep emotion, I extend my heartfelt appreciation to each of you who has joined me on this journey.

With sincere warmth, I invite you to revisit the steps we have taken together through the pages of my earlier works. Our odyssey began with "Journey of Soul - Karma," a book that marked my first foray into the world of words and a testament to the raw passion that ignited my writing adventure.

The subsequent chapters of our shared journey unfolded through the enchanting tapestry of the *"Twenty + One"* series. With each page turned, it felt as though a brushstroke was added to the canvas of our collective imagination—stories and sentiments woven to echo within the quiet corners of your heart. These weren't just words; they were invitations to feel, to reflect, and to remember what truly matters.

And how can I not cherish the transformative path we walked together through the *"Life Changing Journey—Inspirational Quotes Series?"* Day by day, quote by quote, we ventured inward—into spaces often overlooked—to find wisdom in simplicity and light in life's shadows. Each reflection was offered as a gentle whisper of hope, a spark meant to uplift, inspire, and remind us that even in silence, the soul speaks.

The release of "Death - Light of Life and the Shadow of Death" promises to shed new light on the timeless mystery of death. Similarly, "Unleashing the Incredible Potential of Programming with Python - Optimum - PYTHON: Ultimate Guide for Beginners Series I" is poised to empower readers with newfound knowledge.

In addition, my technical book, OPTIMUM Python Series II - Exploring Data Structures and Algorithms, delves into advanced concepts in Python programming, offering a comprehensive guide for those seeking to deepen their understanding.

OPTIMUM – Python Power Series III is your essential guide to mastering the most powerful Python libraries for data science. From data manipulation and visualization to machine learning, this book empowers you with practical tools to solve real-world challenges. Unleash your potential and transform the way you work with data.

Shree Shambav expands his artistic repertoire with "*Whispers of Eternity: 150 Plus - A Symphony of Soulful Verses*," a heartfelt exploration of the human experience. Alongside this, his "*Whispers of the Soul: A Journey Through Haiku*" distils profound insights into poignant verses. Together, these works showcase his versatility and mastery of soulful expression, inviting readers on a journey of self-discovery. Through his poetry, he weaves a rich tapestry of emotion that resonates deeply with the heart.

Shree Shambav's latest works—*Learn to Love Yourself: A Journey of Discovering Inner Beauty and Strength Through 10 Transformative Rules, The Power of Letting Go: Embrace Freedom and Happiness, A Journey of Lasting Peace—are true treasures of self-discovery, The Entitlement Trap: Get Over It, Get On, Whispers of a Dying Soul: Unspoken Regrets and Unlived Dreams, Whispers of Silence - Unlocking Inner Power through Stillness, The Power of Words: Transforming Speech, Transforming Lives, The Art of Intentional Living: Minimalism for a Life of Purpose, Awakening the Infinite:The Power of Consciousness in Transforming Life, Beyond the Veil: A Journey Through Life After Death series, Bonds Beyond Blood - Where love builds bridges, and bonds defy blood., and A Journey into Spiritual Maturity - 12 Golden Rules for Inner Transformation.*

In addition to these works, Shree Shambav has recently ventured into astrology with the release of Astrology Unveiled – Foundations of Ancient

Wisdom Series I to VI, expanding into the realm of metaphysics. These books explore the foundational principles of Vedic astrology, offering readers a rich and practical understanding of this ancient wisdom.

Your unwavering support, enthusiasm to immerse yourself in my writings, and readiness to embark on these journeys with me have been my greatest sources of inspiration. Your input has been a beacon guiding me through the creation process, moulding these stories into containers of passion, emotion, knowledge, and resonance.

As I unveil this new narrative before you, know that your presence, insights, and shared moments have been my companions. The path we have walked together is etched in the annals of my creative evolution, and it's an honour beyond words to have you by my side once more.

Here's to the readers who have illuminated my path with their presence, who have embraced my stories with open hearts, and who have woven themselves into the very fabric of my literary world. Our journey has been a symbiotic dance of writer and reader, a harmony of souls brought together by the magic of storytelling.

With a heart brimming with appreciation and eyes glistening with anticipation, I extend my deepest gratitude for your unwavering support. Thank you for the memories, the shared emotions, and the countless hours spent in the worlds we've crafted together. As we step into this new adventure, let's continue to explore, feel, and discover the boundless horizons that words can unveil.

Warmly,

Shree Shambav

Suggested Reads

FROM BEST-SELLING AUTHOR

Endorsements

"The Inner Battlefield is a transformative guide for anyone seeking clarity, strength, and liberation from the unseen forces that hold us back. Shree Shambav weaves together ancient wisdom and modern insight, creating a profound narrative that challenges and inspires readers to embark on their own journey of self-discovery.

This book doesn't just diagnose the inner enemies—it equips you with practical tools and reflective questions to conquer them. It's not merely a self-help book; it's a spiritual compass that points toward a life of meaning, resilience, and freedom. If you've ever felt trapped by fear, anger, doubt, or desire, this is the battle plan you've been waiting for. A must-read for spiritual seekers and anyone ready to confront their inner demons and emerge victorious."

— Uma Devi, Entrepreunuer

About the Author

Shree Shambav is an internationally acclaimed best-selling author, inspirational speaker, artist, philanthropist, life coach, and entrepreneur. A world record holder, his deep passion for music led him to create soul-stirring albums, drawing inspiration from his celebrated poetry collection, Whispers of Eternity. His profound insights have sparked deep personal transformations, guiding countless individuals toward self-discovery, purposeful living, and authenticity.

With an extraordinary ability to unlock human potential, Shree empowers individuals to break through limitations and embrace their highest selves.

His writings, lectures, and compassionate guidance continue to uplift lives, fostering resilience, mindfulness, and personal growth.

Shree Shambav is a 30x best-selling author celebrated for his profound contributions to personal development and spiritual growth.

Shree Shambav's literary journey took flight with the celebrated Journey of Soul - Karma, where he delved into the depths of human experience to unveil profound insights. Garnering recognition through multiple literature awards, his repertoire includes esteemed works, such as the Twenty + One Series, and the enlightening Life Changing Journey – Inspirational Quotes series.

As a distinguished alumnus of the Indian Institute of Management and the National Institute of Technology, Shree Shambav brings a wealth of corporate acumen from his tenure in multinational corporations. His most recent publications, including Unveiling the Enigma, Death - Light of Life and the Shadow of Death and Optimum – Power Python Series I, Series II and Series III, demonstrate his mastery of both the literary and technical spheres.

Shree Shambav expands his artistic repertoire with "*Whispers of Eternity: 150 Plus - A Symphony of Soulful Verses*," a heartfelt exploration of the human experience. Alongside this, his "*Whispers of the Soul: A Journey Through Haiku*" distils profound insights into poignant verses. Together, these works showcase his versatility and mastery of soulful expression, inviting readers on a journey of self-discovery. Through his poetry, he weaves a rich tapestry of emotion that resonates deeply with the heart.

Shree Shambav's latest works—*Learn to Love Yourself: A Journey of Discovering Inner Beauty and Strength Through 10 Transformative Rules, The Power of Letting Go: Embrace Freedom and Happiness, A Journey of Lasting Peace—are true treasures of self-discovery, The Entitlement Trap: Get Over It, Get On, Whispers of a Dying Soul: Unspoken Regrets and Unlived Dreams, Whispers of Silence - Unlocking Inner Power through Stillness, The Power of Words: Transforming Speech, Transforming Lives, The Art of Intentional Living: Minimalism for a Life of Purpose, Awakening the Infinite:The Power of Consciousness in Transforming Life, Beyond the Veil: A Journey Through Life After Death series, Bonds Beyond Blood - Where love builds bridges, and bonds defy blood., and A Journey into Spiritual Maturity - 12 Golden Rules for Inner Transformation.*

In addition to these works, Shree Shambav has recently ventured into astrology with the release of Astrology Unveiled – Foundations of Ancient Wisdom Series I to VI, expanding into the realm of metaphysics. These books explore the foundational principles of Vedic astrology, offering readers a rich and practical understanding of this ancient wisdom.

Shree Shambav established the Ayur Rakshita Foundation, which is dedicated to promoting boundless growth, universal fraternity, and environmental protection. The charity helps diverse communities while working for societal progress.

To learn more about Shree Shambav and his works, visit his website at www.shambav.org. For information about the Ayur Rakshita Foundation and its initiatives, visit www.shambav-ayurrakshita.org.

Let's Follow him on Social Media: **@shreeshambav**

PREFACE

Life is not merely a series of external victories and defeats—it is an inner journey, a deeply personal struggle where the fiercest battles are often fought in silence. While the world measures success in wealth, power, or recognition, the true measure of a life well-lived lies in the quiet triumph over the enemies that reside within our minds and souls. These adversaries—desire, anger, greed, attachment, pride, jealousy, fear, doubt, guilt, and resistance—are not strangers to any of us. They are the shadows that obscure the light of our potential, the weights that hold us back from living authentically and freely.

The Inner Battlefield: Overcoming the Enemies of the Mind and Soul is a call to arms, not against the world, but against these unseen foes that lurk within each of us. It is an invitation to embark on a journey of self-discovery, to delve into the depths of your being, and to face these inner adversaries with courage, wisdom, and compassion.

This book is not merely a guide—it is a mirror, reflecting the universal human struggle that transcends time, culture, and circumstance. Through the story of a seeker navigating the labyrinth of the self, it offers a framework for understanding the nature of these inner enemies and the tools to overcome them. It reminds us that while these battles are deeply personal, the truths we uncover along the way are universal.

Every chapter of this book is a step into the unknown—a deeper exploration of the mind and soul. Each question posed is an invitation to pause, reflect, and confront the realities we often avoid. The path is not easy; the journey demands honesty, perseverance, and vulnerability. Yet, as you progress, you will find that these struggles are not obstacles but stepping stones leading to liberation, growth, and self-mastery.

We live in a world that constantly pulls us outward, demanding our attention and energy. Yet, true peace and fulfilment can only be found when we turn inward and face what lies within. This book is not about perfection—it is about progress. It is about learning to embrace our flaws, transform our fears, and transcend the illusions that keep us trapped.

As you hold this book in your hands, know that you are not alone in your battles. Each of us carries within us the same enemies and the same potential for victory. The journey may be solitary, but the destination unites us all: a life of freedom, wisdom, and purpose.

May this book serve as your companion and guide, lighting the way as you navigate your own inner battlefield. Remember, the real war is within, and when you win it, you win everything.

With gratitude and encouragement,

Shree Shambav

INTRODUCTION

The real war is within—win it, and you win everything.

In the silence of the night, when the world around us is still, the mind awakens, replaying battles we have fought and those yet to come. These battles are not waged with swords or shields; they are not won by armies or strategies. These are the battles within—the wars of the soul, fought on the inner battlefield where unseen enemies lurk. The conflict is as ancient as humanity itself, yet its relevance remains timeless.

Every day, we face the silent adversaries that dwell within us—desires that chain us, anger that consumes us, greed that blinds us, attachments that deceive us, pride that distances us, and jealousy that poisons our hearts. Beyond these, we confront fear, doubt, guilt, and the resistance to truth. These enemies are not external foes—they are part of us, born from our own thoughts, emotions, and perceptions. They are both the chains that bind us and the teachers that show us the way to freedom.

The Inner Battlefield: Overcoming the Enemies of the Mind and Soul is a journey into the depths of the human spirit. Through the eyes of a young seeker who awakens to the realisation that the real war lies within, this book offers a guide to understanding and overcoming these inner adversaries. Each chapter unveils a specific enemy, shedding light on its nature, its impact, and the path to transcend it.

Part One: The Call to Battle

The journey begins with *The Awakening*, where the seeker realises that something is holding him back from true fulfilment. Guided by a wise mentor, he discovers that the enemies he must defeat are not outside him but within. This realisation marks the start of his inner journey and sets the stage for the battles ahead.

Part Two: The Six Shadows of the Mind

This section explores the six core enemies—*Kama* (Desire), *Krodha* (Anger), *Lobha* (Greed), *Moha* (Attachment), *Mada* (Pride), and *Matsarya* (Jealousy). Each chapter examines how these shadows manifest in our lives, how they deceive and enslave us, and how we can transform them into stepping stones toward growth. From transforming desire into devotion to turning jealousy into inspiration, this section reveals the tools needed to confront these universal struggles.

Part Three: The Final Battle – Beyond the Six Enemies

The journey deepens as the seeker confronts subtler

yet equally destructive enemies—*Fear*, which paralyses; *Doubt*, which keeps us stuck; *Guilt*, which chains us to the past; and *Resistance*, which blinds us to truth. Each chapter in this section goes beyond identifying these adversaries to explore how they can be overcome with courage, faith, self-forgiveness, and self-awareness.

Part Four: The Victory – Discovering the Truth

In the final chapter, the seeker faces his ultimate test, finding liberation and discovering the truth that lies beyond all fears and illusions. The victory is not the end of the journey but the beginning of a life lived with wisdom, love, and purpose. This section inspires the reader to maintain awareness and continue the battle with resilience and grace.

The chapters in this book are not just stories or lessons; they are mirrors reflecting the universal struggles we all face. They invite you to reflect on your own inner enemies and equip you with the wisdom to confront them. This book is not about perfection—it is about progress. It is about awakening to the battles within and embracing the journey toward inner freedom.

As you turn these pages, you will find that the greatest enemy is often yourself, but so is the greatest ally. The battlefield is vast, but the victory is profound. The question is not whether the battle exists—it does. The question is, are you ready to fight? If you are, let this book be your guide, your companion, and your call to arms.

Let the journey begin.

With warmth and sincerity,

Shree Shambav

PROLOGUE

The fiercest battles are not fought on distant fields but within the depths of our own minds.

It begins in silence—an unease that whispers in the quiet moments of life, a restless yearning that no accomplishment or possession can seem to satisfy. There is no external enemy to blame, no visible adversary to conquer. Yet, the struggle is undeniable, an invisible war that rages within. This war is universal, timeless, and deeply personal. It spares no one, not the wealthy, the learned, the devout, or the ordinary. It is the war of the soul—the battle for freedom from the chains of our own making.

The battlefield lies within us, unseen yet relentless. It is here, in the heart of every human being, that the forces of light and shadow clash. Desires pull us toward fleeting pleasures, only to leave us yearning for more. Anger burns, destroying relationships and consuming peace. Greed whispers of endless acquisition, while attachment clings to the impermanent, leaving us adrift when life changes. Pride blinds us with illusions of superiority, and jealousy eats away at our joy. Beyond these, fear shackles us, doubt paralyses us, and guilt drags us into the depths of self-condemnation.

These enemies do not wear uniforms or wield weapons. They are subtle, insidious, and deeply rooted in the fabric of our thoughts and emotions. They do not announce their arrival; they dwell in the shadows, growing stronger with every unexamined action, every unconscious reaction. We try to fight them with distraction, denial, or indulgence, but they return, stronger and more persistent. It is not enough to evade them. To truly find peace, we must face them.

This book is a journey into that battlefield, a guide to identifying and overcoming the enemies of the mind and soul. Through the lens of a young seeker's story, it mirrors the struggles, triumphs, and revelations that define the human experience. The seeker's journey is our journey—an exploration of the inner terrain that challenges us to confront our deepest fears and limitations.

As you embark on this journey, you will meet the shadows that dwell within you. They may seem daunting, even insurmountable, but remember this: the shadows exist only because there is light. And within you lies the power to bring that light to every dark corner of your being.

This book is not just about understanding these inner enemies—it is about transforming them. Desire can be channelled into purpose, anger into strength, greed into generosity. Pride can give way to humility, and jealousy can be replaced with inspiration. Even fear, doubt, and guilt can be turned into stepping stones toward self-awareness and growth. The battle is not easy, but it is worthwhile. For beyond the struggle lies a freedom so profound, it defies words—a life lived with clarity, wisdom, and love.

This is not a call to arms but a call to awareness. It is an invitation to step into the arena of your own soul, to confront what has been holding you back, and to discover the limitless potential that lies beyond. The enemies within are not invincible—they thrive on ignorance and fear, and they wither in the light of truth and understanding.

As you turn these pages, may you find the courage to face your inner battlefield, the wisdom to recognise your true self, and the strength to emerge victorious. For in conquering the enemies within, you will find that the greatest victory is not over others but over the limitations that have kept you from becoming the person you were always meant to be.

The battle begins now. Are you ready to fight?

CONTENTS

At Kumbhariyur

Whispers of the Mist

"The fiercest battles are fought in silence—against the enemies of our own mind. Victory is not in defeating them once, but in rising daily with love, wisdom, and resolve."

- Shree Shambav

The morning in Kumbhariyur was poetry in motion, a symphony of elements that held an almost sacred stillness. The village, nestled in the embrace of ancient hills, seemed to awaken slowly, as if reluctant to disturb the profound quiet of dawn. There was a wisdom to this stillness, an ageless presence that seemed to watch over the land with the patience of a sage. Bhavya stood apart from the others, her figure silhouetted against the soft light breaking through the fog. While the group bustled to ward off the cold, Bhavya lingered, her eyes fixed on the horizon where the first golden rays pierced the mist. It was a moment suspended in time—a breath of eternity amidst the ephemeral.

The air vibrated with life: the distant roar of a waterfall, the faint melody of birdcalls, and the deep hum of frogs that seemed to echo from the very earth. Yet, it was the silence that spoke most powerfully to Bhavya, wrapping her in a cocoon of introspection.

"Bhavya, you'll freeze if you stay there any longer," Akshaya called, his voice warm with care. Vasudeva, standing nearby, nodded in agreement, his breath visible in the crisp air.

Bhavya turned, her cheeks flushed from the chill, a soft smile playing on her lips. "I was just thinking," she said, her voice quiet yet resonant, "this fog... it reminds me of our lives sometimes."

The group began to gather around her—Nita, Lalitha, Sujitha, and others who had arrived for the retreat. They were joined by new faces, each seeking something intangible yet vital, something they couldn't quite articulate but knew they needed.

"What do you mean?" Padma asked, her curiosity piqued.

Bhavya moved closer to an ancient tree that stood like a sentinel in their midst. Its roots twisted and tangled beneath the surface, unseen yet unyielding, while its branches stretched skyward, vast and graceful. She traced the bark with her fingertips, her expression contemplative.

"This tree," she began, her voice gentle but deliberate, "it's like us. Its roots are deeply entwined, drawing from a common source, yet each root battles its own obstacles to grow, just as we do with our inner enemies—anger, greed, desire, fear..."

Kieron, who had just joined the group, greeted everyone warmly. "I've been anxiously waiting for this retreat," he confessed, his excitement blending with the quiet reverence of the moment.

Nita stepped forward, her eyes distant as she shared a memory. "One day, while walking through a meadow, I came across an old man. He was sitting alone, strumming a weathered string instrument. The music was hauntingly beautiful, yet there was no one around to hear it."

Out of curiosity, Nita had asked the man, "Why are you playing this instrument when no one is here to listen?"

The old man had smiled, his eyes twinkling with an inner light. "I play to keep my enemies away," he had replied simply before returning to his music.

"I didn't understand his words at the time," Nita admitted, "until Guruji explained that our inner enemies—anger, greed, desire—are constant companions. The battle against them is ongoing, but with awareness and practice, we can keep them at bay. Victory isn't a moment; it's a way of living—with wisdom, love, and purpose."

The group fell silent, her words sinking deep into their hearts like seeds finding fertile soil. The fog had nearly lifted by now, and the sunlight streamed through the trees, painting the world in hues of gold and amber.

Akshaya broke the silence, his voice thoughtful. "It's remarkable how something as ordinary as a foggy morning or an entangled root can teach us so much about clarity and resilience."

Nita nodded, her eyes reflecting the brilliance of the dawn. "Life is always teaching," she said softly. "It whispers through the fog, sings through the birds, and reveals itself in every sunrise. We just have to pause long enough to hear it."

The tree above them creaked gently, as if affirming her words. It stood as a silent witness to countless mornings like this one, its branches reaching for the heavens while its roots anchored it firmly to the earth.

As the group prepared to move on, Kiran glanced at his watch, a smile tugging at his lips. "Time to get ready for today's session," he reminded them, his practical words blending seamlessly into the tranquil rhythm of the morning.

With light laughter and lingering smiles, the group began their journey back, their footsteps purposeful yet unhurried. They carried with them more than just the beauty of Kumbhariyur's misty morning—they carried its essence. The village had etched itself into their hearts, its timeless wisdom mingling with their own hopes and reflections.

And as the last traces of fog vanished, leaving the path ahead bathed in warm sunlight, it felt as though the land itself had exhaled, releasing them into the day with a quiet blessing. In their hearts, the morning's lessons lingered, waiting to bloom into something transformative, something eternal.

PART ONE

The Call to Battle

"The inner battlefield is not a place of despair but of possibility—where every struggle is an invitation to rise beyond the shadows of the self."

- *Shree Shambav*

CHAPTER I

The Awakening

"The enemies within do not seek to destroy us outright; they thrive in our ignorance, growing stronger when we look away from the truth of who we are."

- Shree Shambav

Synopsis:

In The Awakening, the journey begins as a group of seekers gathers under the guidance of Guruji Shree Shambav. Guruji unveils the concept of the inner battlefield, a sacred yet tumultuous space within every human being. Here, unseen enemies—such as anger, greed, fear, doubt, and attachment—wage a relentless war, often unnoticed yet deeply impactful. Guruji's teachings emphasise the peril of ignoring these internal struggles, warning that unchecked battles lead to chaos, suffering, and a fragmented self. Through his compassionate guidance, the devotees learn that awareness is the first step to mastery. With each revelation, they take a step closer to transformation, igniting a flame of courage, introspection, and purpose within their hearts.

As the serene air settled within the hallowed walls of Shambav Hall, it felt as though time itself had paused to honor the sacredness of the moment. The quiet was not mere silence—it was alive, brimming with an ancient wisdom, as if the very walls, steeped in countless prayers and meditations, cradled the stillness like a vigilant guardian of peace. Outside, the golden rays of the sun filtered softly through the latticework of the windows, painting the floor with intricate patterns that shifted gently, as if divine hands were at play. The room exuded a timeless simplicity, yet it seemed to vibrate with an unseen energy, a sacred hum that calmed restless thoughts and opened the heart to infinite possibilities.

The devotees waited with quiet anticipation, their breaths almost synchronised with the rhythm of the hall's tranquil aura. Each of them had come with a purpose—some seeking answers, others searching for solace, and still others simply yearning for the presence of their Guruji. There was no need for words; the unspoken bond of shared devotion wove them into a collective tapestry of faith and surrender.

And then, as if responding to the unuttered prayers in the room, the doors of Shambav Hall opened. Guruji Shree Shambav entered with an air of profound calm, his every step a meditation in motion. The devotees rose in unison, their reverence palpable. It was not merely a physical act but an offering of their deepest respect, their hearts bowing even before their bodies could. Guruji greeted them with "Atma Namaskar," his voice as gentle as the breeze that carried the fragrance of fresh jasmine into the hall. His hands, raised in a gesture of divine acknowledgment, seemed to gather the collective energies of the room and return them tenfold in peace.

Seating himself in his asana with effortless grace, Guruji closed his eyes. A profound silence descended upon the room—not the silence of emptiness but the silence of presence, the kind that spoke louder than words ever could. It was a stillness that invited each soul to turn inward, to listen to the whispers of the heart and the echoes of the eternal.

Minutes passed, though time felt irrelevant in the embrace of that sacred quiet. The sunlight continued its gentle dance, casting ever-changing patterns that seemed to mirror the inner transformation quietly unfolding within each devotee. And then, as softly as a petal falls, Guruji opened his eyes. The room, already hushed, seemed to hold its breath, awaiting the wisdom that would flow forth—a wisdom not just meant to be heard, but to be felt, absorbed, and lived.

In that moment, the hall was not merely a physical space—it was a sanctuary where the infinite met the finite, where the ordinary was imbued with the extraordinary, and where the journey to the inner battlefield was about to begin.

Apeksha asked, "Guruji, what is the 'inner battlefield,' and why is it significant?"

"The 'inner battlefield,'" Guruji began, his voice low yet resonant, "is not a place of war in the conventional sense. It is the Kurukshetra within—the field where the Pandavas and Kauravas of your soul collide." His reference to the Mahabharata, the ancient Hindu epic, immediately awakened a shared understanding among the devotees. "Just as Arjuna hesitated on the battlefield of Kurukshetra, unsure of his duty, so too do we hesitate when faced with the battles within ourselves—battles against anger, greed, pride, and delusion."

The devotees leaned in, their breaths synchronised with the wisdom unfolding before them.

"In Buddhism," Guruji continued, "this battlefield is likened to the Eightfold Path, where the war is against ignorance, craving, and attachment. Siddhartha Gautama sat beneath the Bodhi tree and fought his own Mara, the tempter, who sought to cloud his awareness. The Buddha's victory was not one of swords or shields but of clarity, mindfulness, and surrender to truth."

Guruji's words painted a vivid picture, weaving threads of wisdom from various traditions. "In Christianity," he said, "the Apostle Paul spoke of the 'armour of

God'—the belt of truth, the breastplate of righteousness, the shield of faith. The inner battlefield here is the constant wrestling between the flesh and the spirit, between temptation and divine purpose. 'For we wrestle not against flesh and blood, but against principalities, against powers, against the rulers of the darkness of this world,' Paul said."

As Guruji paused, the room seemed to hold its breath, the silence deepening like a sacred well. Then, with a gentle smile, he continued, "Sufism speaks of this battlefield as the greater jihad—not a holy war against others, but a holy war within. Rumi wrote, 'When you let go of who you are, you become who you might be.' The Sufi mystic wages a battle not to conquer others but to dissolve the ego, to merge into divine love."

"The Tao," Guruji added, "teaches us that victory in the inner battlefield is achieved through stillness and harmony. Lao Tzu said, 'He who conquers others is strong, he who conquers himself is mighty.' The Taoist sage does not resist the flow of life but surrenders to it, finding strength in softness, clarity in simplicity."

The sunlight, shifting slightly as the morning advanced, now bathed Guruji's serene face in a warm glow. He gestured toward the ancient tree visible through the open window. "In Jainism," he said, "this inner war is against the passions—anger, pride, deceit, and greed—that cloud the soul and bind it to samsara, the cycle of birth and rebirth. The Tirthankaras, the great spiritual teachers, showed us that non-violence, both outwardly and inwardly, is the path to liberation."

Guruji then turned his gaze back to Apeksha, his eyes shimmering like still waters reflecting the sky. "The inner battlefield is significant because it is where we confront our true selves. It is not a place we can avoid; it is woven into the fabric of our existence. If we ignore it, we allow our inner enemies—fear, doubt, ignorance—to grow stronger, binding us tighter in the chains of suffering."

He gestured toward the devotees, his voice filled with compassion. "But this battlefield is also the most sacred space, for it is where the soul awakens. Awareness is the weapon, and guidance—the words of saints, sages, and the whisper of your own conscience—is the map. When Arjuna stood paralysed on Kurukshetra, Krishna guided him not just with teachings but with the profound truth of his inner dharma. Awareness and guidance ignite the journey of transformation."

Guruji, after a pause, said, "The tree, with roots tangled deep in the earth and branches reaching skyward, seemed alive with wisdom. "This tree," he said, "is a reminder. Its roots mirror the complexities of our struggles, but its upward reach reminds us of our purpose: to grow beyond, to rise. The battlefield within is not a curse but a blessing, for it is where we learn to transcend, to connect, and to become."

Akshaya asked, "Guruji, who are the enemies we face in this internal war?"

Guruji closed his eyes briefly, a faint smile gracing his lips. "The enemies we face in this internal war are not external forces, wielding swords or arrows. They are far more insidious and elusive. They reside within us, masquerading as our own thoughts, emotions, and desires. They are anger, greed, envy, attachment, fear, and ignorance. Each one is a shadow cast by our ego, thriving in the dark corners of our mind where awareness is absent."

He paused, his eyes scanning the room, meeting each devotee's gaze as though seeing into their very souls. Then, he leaned forward slightly, his hands resting gently on his knees, and continued.

"Imagine, Akshaya, a grand and ancient fortress," he said. "This fortress is your soul, a place of purity, wisdom, and light. Yet over time, as you live your life, cracks begin to form in its walls. These cracks are born from moments of unawareness—when anger flares, when greed whispers temptations, when fear chains you, or when ignorance blinds you to your true nature.

Through these cracks, the enemies seep in, not as warriors in plain sight, but as invisible infiltrators."

The room was utterly still now, the air thick with the weight of Guruji's words. He continued, weaving an analogy that drew the devotees deeper into the truth.

"Think of anger, for example, as a wildfire. It begins with a single spark—a harsh word, a perceived injustice, or an unmet expectation. Left unchecked, it spreads, consuming everything in its path, reducing the lush forest of your inner peace to ash. Greed, on the other hand, is like a bottomless vessel. No matter how much you pour into it—wealth, possessions, or power—it remains empty, leaving you exhausted and hollow."

He gestured toward the ancient banyan tree outside, its sprawling roots visible even from within the hall. "And attachment," Guruji said, "is like those roots. It binds you to the material world, to people, possessions, and even ideas. While roots give life to a tree, when overgrown, they can entangle and strangle it. Similarly, attachment chokes your spirit, preventing you from growing and reaching toward the light."

Akshaya, his brow furrowed in thought, asked softly, "Guruji, if these enemies are within us, how do we fight them? They seem so deeply rooted, so much a part of who we are."

Guruji smiled. "Ah, my child, the battle is not fought with force but with awareness. It is not about destroying these enemies, for they are part of your human experience. Instead, it is about transforming them. Anger, when understood, can become clarity and courage. Fear can become caution and humility. Even greed, when tamed, can lead to generosity and abundance."

Guruji said, "The battlefield is not out there; it is within. And just as the sun chases away the darkness, awareness chases away ignorance. Through meditation, self-reflection, and the guidance of wisdom, you shine the light of understanding into the shadows of your mind."

The devotees sat in silent contemplation, each absorbing Guruji's words in their own way. Some closed their eyes, their lips moving silently, as if repeating a prayer. Others stared at the ground, lost in their thoughts, their brows furrowed with the weight of revelation.

Guruji's voice softened, as though he were speaking not just to the group but to each soul individually. "The inner battlefield is not a place of despair, but of possibility. Each struggle you face is an invitation to grow, to rise beyond the shadows of the self, and to align with your highest truth. This war is not one of destruction but of liberation—a journey from darkness to light, from ignorance to wisdom, from bondage to freedom."

As his words settled over the room like a gentle rain, Akshaya felt a quiet resolve stir within him. The enemies Guruji spoke of no longer seemed invincible; they were challenges, yes, but not unconquerable. For the first time, he saw the inner battlefield not as a place of endless strife, but as sacred ground where transformation was possible.

Roopa asked, "What happens if we ignore these struggles?"

Roopa's question fell into the stillness of Shambav Hall like a pebble into a serene pond, rippling through the air and stirring the thoughts of all present. Guruji, seated in quiet grace, looked at her with an expression that blended compassion and gravity.

For a moment, Guruji's gaze drifted to the ancient banyan tree outside, its roots sprawling deep into the earth and its branches reaching endlessly toward the heavens. He sighed softly, as though the weight of Roopa's question brought forth the echoes of countless lives lived in avoidance, in ignorance, and in silent suffering. Then he spoke, his voice calm yet carrying a depth that pierced the heart.

"Roopa," Guruji began, his words flowing like the gentle current of a sacred river, "to ignore these struggles is to turn our backs on the very purpose of life. It is to let the weeds of ignorance overtake the garden of our soul. Like a farmer who neglects his field, we may initially convince ourselves that all is well—that the crops will grow on their own. But over time, the weeds creep in. They choke the life out of the fertile soil, and soon, what could have been a lush harvest becomes barren, lifeless."

He paused, letting the metaphor take root in their minds. The devotees sat motionless, their breaths synchronised with the rhythm of his words.

"When we ignore these inner struggles—our anger, our attachments, our fears—they do not simply vanish," Guruji continued. "Instead, they grow stronger, like a fire left unattended. They spread into the hidden corners of our hearts and minds, consuming our joy, our peace, and even our sense of purpose. The enemies within thrive in the darkness of ignorance, feeding on our denial. And before we know it, we become strangers to ourselves—living lives shaped not by our highest aspirations, but by the shadows we have refused to confront."

His eyes locked onto Roopa's, his gaze penetrating yet gentle, like a father speaking directly to his child's soul. "Imagine, Roopa, a majestic ship sailing the ocean. This ship represents your life, your journey. Now imagine ignoring the tiny holes in its hull. At first, the damage seems minor—just a few trickles of water seeping in. But over time, the water accumulates, unseen and unaddressed, until one day the ship begins to sink. That, is what happens when we ignore our inner battles. We may appear to float on the surface for a while, but deep within, we are drowning."

Roopa swallowed hard, her lips trembling as the weight of Guruji's words pressed upon her. The other devotees, too, shifted slightly, as if his imagery had awakened something dormant within them—a quiet recognition of the battles they had ignored, the wounds they had left untended.

Guruji's voice softened, but the intensity of his message deepened. "The ancient texts speak of this. In the Bhagavad Gita, Arjuna stood on the battlefield, trembling with doubt and fear, wishing to turn away from the fight before him. But Krishna, his guide, reminded him that to turn away is not to escape. It is to prolong the suffering, to let the enemies of the mind—despair, confusion, and ignorance—claim victory without resistance. Life itself is the Kurukshetra, the battlefield. And to live fully, we must engage in this sacred war, not to destroy but to transform."

"The Buddha taught this as well," Guruji continued. "He called it the path of mindfulness—bringing awareness to our suffering, not avoiding it. To ignore is to perpetuate samsara, the endless cycle of birth, death, and rebirth, driven by unresolved karma and unacknowledged desires. But when we face our struggles, when we bring the light of awareness to our darkest corners, we step onto the path of liberation."

The hall was silent except for the faint rustling of leaves outside, as if the banyan tree itself was nodding in agreement. Roopa, her eyes glistening, whispered, "But Guruji, it seems so overwhelming. How do we even begin?"

Guruji smiled—a gentle, knowing smile that carried the promise of hope. "You begin by acknowledging that the struggle exists. That is the first and most courageous step. You begin by seeking guidance, by cultivating awareness, and by remembering that you are not alone. Even the mightiest tree began as a seed. Even the brightest flame started as a spark."

He pointed to the flickering oil lamp that burned at the centre of the hall, its flame steady yet alive, as though mirroring his words. "And you begin, Roopa, by trusting the process. Just as the lamp burns away the oil to give light, so too must we burn away our illusions, our fears, and our attachments. It is not easy, but it is sacred. It is the journey from ignorance to wisdom, from fear to love, from darkness to light."

The devotees sat in profound stillness, the weight of Guruji's words settling into their hearts like seeds into fertile soil. Roopa bowed her head, her hands trembling as they came together in a gesture of reverence. "Thank you, Guruji," she whispered, her voice thick with emotion. "I will not ignore these struggles anymore."

Guruji nodded. "Good," he said softly. "Remember, the inner battlefield is not a place of despair but of transformation. It is where you confront not your enemies but the shadows of yourself. And in doing so, you discover the infinite light within."

Akshatha asked, "How can awareness and guidance ignite the journey to transformation?"

"Ah, Akshatha," he said, his tone carrying both affection and solemnity, "awareness and guidance—these are not mere tools for transformation; they are the very flames that ignite it. Without them, the soul remains in slumber, like a lotus hidden beneath murky waters, waiting for the first rays of light to awaken its bloom."

He gestured toward the oil lamp burning at the center of the hall, its flame steady and unwavering. "Awareness," he began, "is like the wick of this lamp. It is the foundation, the thread that connects the soul to the divine spark within. But a wick alone cannot shine. It requires the fire of guidance to bring it to life, to illuminate its purpose. Together, they create the flame—the flame that pierces the darkness of ignorance and reveals the path ahead."

The devotees sat in rapt attention, their breaths synchronised with the rhythm of his words. Guruji leaned forward slightly, his hands resting gently on his knees. "Let me share a story," he said, his voice softening to an almost whisper-like cadence. "A story from the ancient Upanishads, where a young seeker named Nachiketa stood at the gates of Yama, the god of death. Nachiketa was filled with questions—questions about life, death, and the eternal truth. He was aware of his own ignorance, and it was this awareness that gave him the courage to seek answers. But it was the guidance of Yama, the divine teacher, that ignited his journey to self-realisation. Yama did not simply hand him the truth; he lit the lamp of understanding within Nachiketa, allowing the boy to see for himself the eternal nature of the soul."

Guruji paused, letting the weight of the story settle into the room. "You see, Akshatha," he continued, "awareness is the recognition that there is more to life than what we perceive. It is the quiet whisper that tells us there is a greater truth, a higher purpose. But guidance—ah, guidance is the hand that steadies us when the path becomes uncertain. It is the wisdom of those who have walked the journey before us, who have faced the same battles and emerged victorious."

"Consider the banyan tree," Guruji said, his voice resonant with metaphor. "The seed contains the potential to become this magnificent giant, but it cannot grow alone. It needs the soil to anchor it, the sun to nourish it, and the rain to sustain it. Awareness is like the seed's awakening—it knows it must grow, and it knows there is a greater purpose within. But guidance is the sun, the rain, the nurturing elements that transform the seed into its fullest potential."

Akshatha's eyes glistened as she listened, her heart absorbing the wisdom like a parched earth drinking in rain. Guruji continued, his voice steady but infused with compassion. "Without awareness, we remain trapped in the cycle of samsara, the endless loop of birth, death, and rebirth. We stumble in the darkness, unable to see the chains that bind us. Without guidance, even if we become aware of these chains, we may not know how to break them. The scriptures, the Guru, the teachings—they are the maps and the light that help us navigate the treacherous terrain of the inner world."

He looked around the hall, his gaze sweeping over the silent, attentive devotees. "In Buddhism, the Buddha himself was called the 'Awakened One,' because he achieved complete awareness. But it was his teachings, his guidance, that illuminated the path for countless others to walk the Middle Way. In Christianity, Jesus said, 'I am the way, the truth, and the life.' His awareness of divine truth was profound, but it was his guidance—his parables, his actions—that lit the way for his disciples. And in Sufism, the guide, the Murshid, is considered indispensable because they help the seeker navigate the labyrinth of the heart."

Guruji's voice softened further, taking on a tone that felt almost like a caress. "Akshatha, imagine a dark cave filled with treasures—a cave that represents the depths of your soul. Awareness is the realisation that the treasures exist, that within you lies untapped wisdom, love, and divinity. But guidance is the torch that illuminates the path through the cave, helping you avoid the pitfalls, the illusions, and the fears that might otherwise lead you astray. Together, they allow you to claim the treasure—to realise your true self."

The room was silent, the kind of silence that speaks volumes. Akshatha bowed her head, her hands trembling slightly as they came together in a gesture of reverence. "Guruji," she said, her voice barely above a whisper, "thank you for showing me the light."

Guruji smiled, a smile that carried the weight of lifetimes and the promise of infinite possibilities. "Remember," he said gently, "the journey to transformation begins not with grand actions but with a simple spark. Be aware of the light within you, and seek the guidance that will help it grow. For in the end, every step you take toward your true self is a step toward the divine."

The devotees sat in stillness, their hearts quietly ignited by the wisdom shared. Outside, the banyan tree swayed gently in the breeze, as though bowing in acknowledgment of the sacred truth that had been spoken.

Guruji, after a long, contemplative silence, opened his eyes slowly and, with a soft smile, said, "Let us take a small break for refreshment." His words seemed to echo like the gentle toll of a temple bell, signaling not just a pause for the body but a moment of reflection for the mind and spirit. The devotees, still immersed in the afterglow of his teachings, stood and quietly filed out of Shambav Hall, the calmness of the sacred space following them like an invisible embrace.

As they stepped outside, the sun was at its zenith, casting its golden rays over the serene ashram grounds. The air was cool and cosy despite the day was sunny, as if nature itself conspired to maintain the sanctuary's tranquillity. A soft breeze caressed their faces, carrying with it the faint, wild fragrance of blooming flowers and the earthy notes of herbs growing along the ashram's edges. The scents mingled, evoking memories of timeless simplicity and natural abundance.

The devotees walked leisurely toward the refreshment counters, where the atmosphere was alive with the comforting aroma of freshly brewed coffee and the buttery sweetness of cookies just out of the oven. The scent seemed to wrap itself around them, drawing them closer with an irresistible warmth. Some chose strong, dark coffee, savouring the bold bitterness that awakened their senses. Others opted for herbal tea, its delicate flavours steeped in the wisdom of ancient remedies, while a few indulged in the simple pleasure of chai, its blend of spices and milk a symphony of comfort.

Akshaya, holding a steaming cup of strong coffee, joined a small group of devotees for a brief stroll along the shaded paths of the ashram. The gravel crunched softly beneath their feet as they wandered through the garden, where marigolds, jasmines, and tulsi plants danced lightly in the breeze. The vibrant colours of the flowers seemed to reflect the joy of the moment, while the quiet hum of bees and the distant chirping of birds added a melodic undertone to their conversation.

They spoke in hushed tones, reflecting on Guruji's teachings and sharing their own insights, their words punctuated by soft laughter and moments of thoughtful silence. Akshaya looked up at the banyan tree, its ancient roots sprawling deeply into the earth and its branches stretching toward the heavens. It stood as a silent witness to countless seekers who had walked the same path before them. "The banyan tree," Akshaya murmured to himself, "a reminder of how deeply rooted we must be in awareness, yet how far we must reach for truth."

After their stroll, the devotees began to make their way back to Shambav Hall, their steps lighter, their hearts more open. The hall, now bathed in the softer light of the afternoon sun, welcomed them like an old friend. The latticework of the windows cast intricate patterns on the marble floor, as if the universe itself had left behind a subtle message in its geometry.

The devotees took their seats once more, the quiet murmur of anticipation filling the room as they awaited Guruji's return. Each one carried with them the stillness of the break—a stillness infused with the wisdom of nature, the warmth of community, and the deepening understanding of their inner journey. The aroma of coffee and chai lingered faintly in the air, mingling with the sacred atmosphere of Shambav Hall, as though even the most mundane moments had been sanctified by their collective purpose.

When Guruji finally entered, his presence brought with it a renewed sense of calm and focus. He greeted the devotees with his gentle Atma Namaskar, his hands forming a gesture of respect that felt like an embrace for each soul present. The devotees straightened in their seats, their attention wholly fixed on him, their hearts ready to absorb the next wave of wisdom.

PART TWO

The Six Shadows of the Mind

"True liberation is not the absence of struggle but the mastery of it—walking through the storm with a steady heart, anchored in truth, and illuminated by love."

- *Shree Shambav*

CHAPTER II

The Enemy of Desire

"The greatest war we face is not with the world outside, but within the quiet corridors of our mind—where our fears, doubts, and desires reside as adversaries, waiting to be understood and transcended."

– Shree Shambav

Synopsis

Overcoming the Enemies of the Mind and Soul, Shree Shambav unveils a transformative journey that delves into the unseen battles within the human mind and spirit. Through the lens of a young devotee's interactions with a wise Guru, the book explores the inner enemies—desire, anger, greed, attachment, pride, and jealousy—and their profound impact on our lives. Blending ancient wisdom with practical insights, this narrative serves as a guide to awakening awareness, embracing self-mastery, and discovering the path to inner peace. Each chapter offers tools for reflection, spiritual growth, and the ultimate victory: liberation from the struggles that cloud our true essence.

Kama - Lust, Excessive Wants

Guruji closed his eyes for a moment. The devotees in Shambav Hall leaned forward slightly, their anticipation palpable. Guruji finally opened his eyes, his gaze warm yet piercing, and spoke softly, "Abhilasha, let me share a story that may help illuminate the answer to your question."

The room seemed to breathe as Guruji began. "There was once a farmer named Anand who lived in a quiet, fertile valley. Anand owned a modest piece of land, enough to sustain his family and provide a simple but fulfilling life. One day, a travelling merchant came through the valley, speaking of a faraway kingdom where gold coins lay scattered on the ground, waiting to be picked up by anyone willing to journey there. The farmer's heart leapt at the thought. What if he could gather enough gold to buy more land, more cattle, and a larger house? Surely then, he would be truly happy."

Guruji paused, his voice steady but filled with undertones of caution. "And so, Anand left his fields behind and embarked on the journey to the golden kingdom. Days turned into weeks and weeks into months as he wandered through forests, crossed rivers, and climbed mountains. Along the way, he encountered challenges—harsh weather, treacherous paths, and hunger. But Anand was undeterred, for he believed that every step brought him closer to happiness. Finally, he reached the kingdom the merchant had described."

The devotees listened intently, their imaginations carrying them to the world of Anand. Guruji's voice softened, drawing them in further. "The rumours were true—the ground was indeed scattered with gold coins. Anand fell to his knees and began scooping them up, his heart racing with excitement. But as the hours passed, he realised something peculiar. No matter how many coins he gathered, his hunger for more only grew. He could not stop. The thought of leaving, even with a heavy sack of gold, filled him with unease. What if there were more coins just around the corner? What if he missed the opportunity to gather even more? Day after day, he toiled, his back bent, his hands blistered, his heart weighed down by the very thing he had believed would make him free."

Guruji's voice grew softer, almost a whisper, as if the lesson itself required quiet reverence. "Anand never returned to his valley. He became a prisoner, not of the gold, but of his own insatiable desire."

The hall was silent, the weight of the story pressing on every heart. Guruji continued, his tone now layered with both compassion and urgency. "Excessive desire is like Anand's pursuit of gold—it blinds us to what we already have, to the beauty and abundance that exists within and around us. Instead of enjoying the fruits of our efforts, we are consumed by the thought of what we do not yet possess. It is like drinking saltwater to quench your thirst—the more you consume, the thirstier you become."

He leaned forward slightly, his gaze sweeping across the room. "Desire in itself is not the enemy. It is natural to want, to strive, and to dream. But excessive desire—the kind that takes over our thoughts and leads us away from contentment—creates suffering. It distracts us from the present moment, where true joy resides. It places our happiness on a distant horizon that always moves further away."

Abhilasha nodded, her eyes glistening with both understanding and a touch of sorrow. "Guruji," she said softly, "are we all Anand in some way?"

Guruji smiled gently, the lines of his face softening, as though he carried infinite compassion for the question. "Yes, Abhilasha. We are all Anand at times. The desires may differ—some chase wealth, others fame, some love, and others validation. But the root is the same. The cure is also the same—awareness. Awareness helps us pause, reflect, and ask ourselves: Is this desire serving my growth or chaining me further? Awareness that brings gratitude for what we already hold in our hearts."

He gestured to the devotees, his voice now steady and grounded. "Think of excessive desire as a fire. It can provide warmth and light when tended to carefully, but if left unchecked, it can consume everything in its path. The key is to cultivate discernment, to know when to feed the fire and when to let it burn out."

The devotees sat in quiet reflection, the weight of Guruji's words settling over them like a soft, warm blanket. Outside, the wind carried the faint scent of flowers into the hall, a gentle reminder of the abundance life already offers.

After a pause, Guruji said, his voice soft yet resolute. "The inner battlefield is not won by extinguishing desire completely, but by transforming it. Let your desires align with your higher self—with love, service, and wisdom. When your desires are rooted in truth, they no longer imprison you. Instead, they become wings, lifting you toward freedom."

Akanksh asked, "Guruji, what distinguishes healthy ambition from destructive craving?"

Guruji smiled gently at Akanksh's question. "Akanksh," Guruji began, his voice calm yet profound, "to understand the difference between healthy ambition and destructive craving, let us think of two rivers flowing toward the same ocean. One river flows steadily, carving its path through the land with purpose and grace, nourishing everything it touches—villages, fields, forests. The other river, however, surges chaotically, flooding its banks, uprooting trees, and sweeping away all in its path. Both rivers are moving toward the same goal, but only one brings life, harmony, and fulfilment to everything it encounters. The other leaves destruction and emptiness in its wake."

He paused, letting the analogy settle in the minds of his audience. Then he continued, "Healthy ambition is like the first river. It flows from a place of purpose and alignment with your higher self. It seeks to grow, to create, and to contribute—not just for personal gain but for the upliftment of all. This kind of ambition brings clarity and joy. It empowers you to achieve great things without losing your connection to the present moment. Healthy ambition asks, 'How can I grow while helping others grow? How can my success serve not just me, but the greater good?'"

Guruji leaned forward slightly, his voice taking on a deeper, more introspective tone. "Destructive craving, on the other hand, is like the second river. It is driven by fear, ego, and an insatiable hunger for more—more power, more possessions, more validation. It blinds us to the needs of others and even to the needs of our own soul. Destructive craving whispers in our ear that nothing is ever enough, that we must always have more to prove our worth, to secure our happiness. But in the end, it leaves us hollow, like a river that dries up after consuming all in its path."

Akanksh nodded slowly, his brow furrowed in thought. "Guruji, how can we recognise when our ambitions are turning into destructive cravings?"

Guruji's face softened with understanding. "This is a profound question, Akanksh, and the answer lies in awareness. Ask yourself: Does my ambition bring me peace, or does it make me restless? Does it inspire me to uplift others, or does it lead me to compare, compete, and isolate? Healthy ambition feels like a steady flame, warming and illuminating. Destructive craving feels like a wildfire, consuming everything in its path, including the one who started it."

He paused, then added with a glimmer of a smile, "The mind often confuses ambition with craving, for the two can look very similar from the outside. Both may drive you to work hard, to strive for greatness. But the energy behind them is what distinguishes one from the other. Healthy ambition arises from love—love for what you do, love for the people you serve, love for the growth it brings. Destructive craving, however, arises from lack—a feeling that you are incomplete, that you must achieve or acquire something to fill a void within."

The hall was silent, but the atmosphere buzzed with introspection. Guruji looked around, as if connecting with each devotee individually, and continued. "Let me share a story."

"There was once a sculptor named Keshav who lived in a small village. He was known far and wide for his exquisite statues, each one a masterpiece of art and devotion. Keshav's dream was to carve a statue of the divine so magnificent that it would inspire anyone who saw it to feel closer to God. For years, he worked tirelessly, chiselling away at a massive block of marble with love and patience. Each strike of his hammer was filled with reverence, each detail crafted with care. When the statue was finally unveiled, it was so breathtaking that people came from distant lands to witness it. Keshav felt a quiet joy, not because of the praise he received, but because he knew his work had served a higher purpose."

Guruji's voice grew quieter, drawing everyone deeper into the story. "But in the same village, there was another sculptor, Vishal, who also dreamed of greatness. Unlike Keshav, Vishal's ambition was driven by a craving for fame and wealth. He, too, began working on a grand statue, but his focus was not on the beauty of the work or the inspiration it might bring to others. Instead, his mind was consumed with thoughts of how many coins it would earn, how many people would call him the greatest sculptor. As he worked, his dissatisfaction grew—no curve was perfect enough, no detail fine enough. His obsession with perfection, born not of love but of fear, caused him to work until his hands bled and his mind unravelled. In the end, the statue remained incomplete, and Vishal was left with nothing but exhaustion and regret."

Guruji's gaze softened, and his voice carried both compassion and clarity. "Keshav and Vishal both started with the same ambition: to create something magnificent. But one was driven by love and devotion, while the other was driven by craving and fear. This is the difference, Akanksh. Healthy ambition creates; destructive craving consumes. Healthy ambition fulfils, destructive craving depletes."

He paused, letting his words settle, and then said, "The key to distinguishing between the two lies in your intention. When your ambition arises from a place of love, it feels expansive, freeing, and joyful. It inspires not just you but everyone around you. But when it arises from craving, it feels constrictive, burdensome, and isolating. Look within, Akanksh, and ask yourself: Does my ambition feel like a steady river or a raging flood? The answer will guide you."

As the devotees sat in quiet contemplation, the scent of wildflowers drifted into the hall as if nature itself had come to affirm the lesson.

Padma asked, "Guruji, how can we transform material desires into a higher purpose?"

Guruji listened intently to Padma's question, his eyes reflecting the depth of her yearning for understanding. After a moment of silence, Guruji began to speak, his voice soft yet powerful, carrying the weight of timeless truths. "Padma," he said, "material desires, like fire, are neither inherently good nor bad. In their raw state, they can consume us, leaving behind ashes of dissatisfaction. But when understood, refined, and redirected, they can become the very fuel that lights the path to a higher purpose."

He paused, letting the analogy settle in their minds. "Let me share a story," he continued, his gaze sweeping across the room, drawing everyone into his words.

"There was once a young boy named Arvind who lived in a small village. Arvind loved jewels—he was fascinated by their brilliance, their colours, and the way they seemed to capture the light of the sun. Every day, he would dream of owning the most precious gems, believing they would bring him happiness and fulfilment. He worked tirelessly, saving every coin, sacrificing small joys in pursuit of his dream. After years of effort, he finally acquired a collection of jewels so exquisite that they dazzled everyone who saw them. Yet, to his surprise, the joy he felt was fleeting. The jewels, once a source of wonder, now seemed heavy in his heart, their luster dimmed by the emptiness within."

Guruji paused, his voice taking on a deeper, more introspective tone. "One day, Arvind encountered a wise sage who saw the burden in his eyes. The sage asked him, 'What do you see when you look at these jewels?' Arvind replied, 'I see beauty and wealth, but they no longer bring me happiness.' The sage smiled and said, 'What if these jewels were not meant to adorn your body but to adorn the lives of others? What if their true purpose is to bring light where there is darkness, to heal where there is pain?'"

The devotees listened intently, their minds captivated by the unfolding story. Guruji continued, "Inspired by the sage's words, Arvind decided to use his jewels to help those in need. He sold the gems and used the wealth to build a school for the children of his village, a place where knowledge and wisdom could shine brighter than any diamond. As he saw the children learning, laughing, and growing, Arvind felt a joy he had never known—a joy that came not from possession but from purpose. In transforming his desire for jewels into a desire to serve, Arvind discovered the true meaning of wealth."

Guruji's eyes sparkled as he leaned forward slightly, his voice carrying both clarity and compassion. "Padma, material desires are like uncut stones. In their raw form, they may seem ordinary or even burdensome. But when we polish them with awareness and purpose, they become jewels that illuminate not just our lives but the lives of others. The key lies in understanding the deeper longing behind our desires. Do we desire wealth? Then ask, 'How can this wealth bring comfort and dignity to others?' Do we desire recognition? Then ask, 'How can my work inspire and uplift the world?' Do we desire love? Then ask, 'How can I give love unconditionally, without expecting it in return?'"

He paused, allowing the depth of his words to sink in. "Transforming material desires into a higher purpose is not about denying or suppressing them. It is about transcending their surface level and uncovering the sacred impulse beneath. Every desire, when examined with honesty and humility, reveals a deeper yearning—for connection, for growth, for meaning. And when we align our desires with the greater good, they become powerful tools for spiritual evolution."

Guruji's gaze softened as he continued, "Think of a kite, Padma. To fly high, it needs both the pull of the wind and the grounding of the string. Material desires are like the wind—they give us the energy to aspire, to move, to grow. But without the string of purpose to guide them, they can scatter us in all directions. Purpose anchors us, ensuring that our aspirations lift us higher without losing connection to the earth, to our roots, to what truly matters."

The hall was silent, but the atmosphere hummed with a profound energy. Padma's eyes glistened with gratitude as she whispered, "Guruji, how do we find this higher purpose?"

Guruji smiled, a gentle warmth radiating from him. "By listening to the whispers of your soul, Padma. Your higher purpose is not something you find outside of you—it is already within, waiting to be uncovered. Begin by asking yourself: What brings me true joy? What gifts have I been given that I can share with the world? What legacy do I wish to leave behind? Let these questions guide you, and trust that every step you take in service of others is a step toward your higher self."

Vasudeva asked, "Guruji, how does detachment create room for true fulfillment?"

Guruji leaned forward slightly, his posture inviting connection. He closed his eyes for a brief moment as if drawing the answer from a sacred reservoir within. Then, with a voice as steady as the rhythm of the tides, he began to speak.

"Vasudeva," Guruji said, "detachment is often misunderstood as indifference or coldness, but it is far from that. Detachment is the art of holding the world lightly yet lovingly, without being consumed by the weight of its outcomes. It is not about renouncing life, but about engaging with it fully, without losing yourself in the process."

He paused, allowing his words to ripple through the room. Then he continued, weaving his response into a story.

"Many years ago, there lived a sculptor named Dhruv, known far and wide for his extraordinary artistry. His sculptures captured not just the physical form but the very essence of life, as though they were whispers of the divine frozen in stone. One day, the king commissioned him to create a grand statue that would adorn the royal courtyard. Dhruv poured his heart into his work, chiselling with precision and love, day after day. When the statue was finally unveiled, it was a masterpiece beyond compare. The king was so moved that he declared Dhruv the finest sculptor in the land."

Guruji's voice grew softer, drawing the devotees deeper into the tale. "But something unexpected happened. Instead of feeling joy, Dhruv felt an emptiness growing within him. He became obsessed with his reputation, fearing that his next work might not measure up. The anxiety of perfection replaced the joy of creation. His art, once a sacred expression, became a burden he could no longer carry."

Guruji's gaze swept across the hall, his words resonating with an unspoken truth. "One day, a wandering monk visited Dhruv. Seeing his turmoil, the monk asked, 'Why do you sculpt?' Dhruv replied, 'To create beauty and to honour the divine.' The monk smiled and said, 'Then why do you cling to the outcomes? The divine does not measure the worth of your creation by its applause but by the purity of your intent. Detach yourself from the result, and you will rediscover the joy of your craft.'"

Guruji leaned back, his voice now carrying the weight of revelation. "Dhruv took the monk's words to heart. He began sculpting again, but this time, he let go of the need for praise or recognition. His hands moved freely, guided by love and devotion. And in that freedom, he found joy once more. His sculptures became more alive than ever, not because he sought perfection, but because he was no longer bound by the chains of expectation."

Guruji turned to Vasudeva, his eyes soft yet piercing. "Detachment, Vasudeva, is the monk's wisdom. It is the ability to create, to love, to act, and to live without the constant need to possess or control the outcome. Imagine holding water in your hands. If you try to grasp it tightly, it slips through your fingers. But if you cup your hands gently, it stays. Life is like that water—when we cling to it, we lose it. When we hold it lightly, it flows through us, nourishing and fulfilling us."

The devotees sat in rapt attention, the analogy etching itself into their hearts. Guruji continued, his voice now a gentle river, carrying them toward deeper understanding. "Detachment creates room for true fulfilment because it frees us from the tyranny of attachment. When we are attached, we live in fear—fear of loss, fear of failure, fear of not being enough. This fear constricts our hearts and clouds our vision. But when we detach, we make space for grace to enter. We become open to life's gifts, receiving them with gratitude and releasing them with love."

Guruji smiled, the light of the setting sun reflecting in his eyes. "Consider a garden, Vasudeva. If a gardener clings to every flower, refusing to let them bloom or wither, the garden becomes stagnant, lifeless. But when the gardener tends to the plants with care, allowing each flower to blossom and fade in its own time, the garden thrives. Detachment is the gardener's wisdom—it lets life unfold in its natural rhythm, bringing beauty and fulfilment in ways we cannot always predict."

Vasudeva's eyes glistened as he absorbed Guruji's words. "Guruji," he asked softly, "how do we cultivate this detachment in our daily lives?"

fulfilmenttoGuruji's face lit up with a serene smile. "By practicing two things, Vasudeva: awareness and surrender. Awareness helps us see the roots of our attachments, how we tie our happiness to external things. Surrender helps us trust the flow of life, knowing that what is meant for us will come and that what leaves us was never truly ours. Together, they transform attachment into freedom, and freedom into fulfillment."

CHAPTER III

The Enemy of Anger

'Life blooms most beautifully when we become gardeners of detachment—nurturing what we have with care but allowing each flower to blossom and fade in its own time."

– Shree Shambav

Synopsis

The profound concept of detachment is explored as Guruji illuminates how letting go of attachment to material outcomes creates space for inner peace and fulfilment. Through the analogy of a sculptor's journey and the wisdom of a wandering monk, Guruji teaches that true freedom arises when we engage with life wholeheartedly but without clinging to its results. The devotees learn that detachment is not about rejecting the world but about embracing it with open hands, allowing life to flow naturally and beautifully. Awareness and surrender become the guiding principles for transforming attachment into liberation, leading to a life of deeper purpose and joy.

Krodha - Wrath, Uncontrolled Rage

Vidyarthi asked, "What lies at the root of anger, and how can we address it?"

As the gentle afternoon light filtered through the lattice of Shambav Hall, the devotees sat quietly, waiting for Guruji's wisdom. There was a tangible stillness in the air, punctuated only by the distant hum of bees outside and the rhythmic rustle of leaves in the breeze. Vidyarthi, seated near the front, raised his hand, his expression one of quiet curiosity mixed with a hint of personal longing. "Guruji," he asked, his voice steady but earnest, "What lies at the root of anger, and how can we address it?"

Guruji looked at Vidyarthi, his eyes filled with the kind of compassion that could hold the weight of a thousand unspoken sorrows. After a brief pause, he began, his voice as calm as a still lake, "Anger, my child, is like a wildfire. It does not ignite on its own but arises from the friction of unmet expectations, wounded ego, and unhealed pain. At its root lies fear—fear of loss, fear of rejection, fear of vulnerability. Anger is the mask that fear wears to appear strong."

The devotees leaned in closer, captivated by his words. Guruji continued, "Imagine a pond, serene and reflective. If a stone is thrown into it, the ripples distort its surface, obscuring its clarity. Anger is that distortion—it clouds our ability to see things as they are. But the stone itself is often our deeper wound: our fear, our insecurity, our unresolved hurt."

He paused, allowing the analogy to settle into their hearts. Then, as if conjuring a memory, he said, "Many years ago, I met a blacksmith in a small village. His hands were calloused, and his face bore the marks of a life lived in toil. I watched as he forged a piece of iron, striking it repeatedly with a hammer, each blow precise yet measured. Intrigued, I asked him, 'Why do you strike the iron so hard when it resists you?' He smiled and replied, 'I am not striking to destroy it, but to shape it into something stronger, more purposeful.'"

Guruji turned his gaze to Vidyarthi. "Anger, like the unshaped iron, must be tempered and understood. If we react with force against our anger, we risk breaking ourselves. But if we approach it with awareness and patience, we can transform it into strength. Just as the blacksmith sees potential in the stubborn iron, we must see the wisdom hidden within our anger."

Vidyarthi's eyes reflected both awe and introspection. Guruji continued, "The first step in addressing anger is to recognise it—not to suppress or deny it but to observe it. When you feel its fire rising within you, ask yourself: What am I afraid of? What pain am I protecting? In this inquiry lies the seed of transformation. With time and mindfulness, you'll find that anger can become a guide—a signal pointing you toward the wounds that need healing."

Guruji leaned forward slightly, his voice taking on a softer, more deliberate tone, as though each word carried the weight of centuries of wisdom. "In the Bhagavad Gita," he began, "Lord Krishna does not condemn anger, nor does he dismiss its existence. Instead, He lays bare its origins and its destructive potential while offering a way to master it. Anger, Krishna says, is not an isolated emotion—it is the offspring of attachment and desire. It is the fire that burns when our cravings remain unfulfilled. Yet, like fire, it can also be harnessed, channeled, and transformed."

He recited Bhagvad Gita Chapter 2 Verse 62the verse, his voice steady and resonant:

dhyaayato vishayaan pumsah sangas teshupajaayate |
sangaat sanjayate kaamah kamat krodho 'bhijaayate | |

Meaning: "While contemplating the objects of the senses, one develops attachment to them. From attachment arises desire, and from desire, anger is born."

Guruji paused, letting the profound simplicity of the verse settle over the devotees. "What Krishna explains is a timeless truth," he continued. "Anger, greed, and lust are not just passing emotions—they are 'manas rog', diseases of the mind. And like any disease, they require awareness and effort to cure."

He leaned back, his eyes scanning the room. "Consider a river," he said, his voice weaving imagery into his words. "When a river flows within its banks, it nurtures life. It irrigates fields, quenches thirst, and sustains ecosystems. But when its banks are breached, the river becomes a flood—destructive, uncontrollable, and devastating. Anger is like that river. Without the banks of awareness and self-restraint, it overflows, destroying relationships, peace, and clarity. But with awareness, that same energy can irrigate the barren fields of our hearts, transforming suffering into strength and wisdom."

He then shared a story that many could relate to. "Imagine a boy named Ramesh," Guruji began. "In his school, he notices a girl, Kavitha. Something about her captures his attention, and soon, he begins to think of her constantly. 'If only she were mine,' he tells himself, over and over again. His mind, consumed by this thought, becomes attached to her. The more he thinks, the stronger the attachment grows, until it transforms into a deep desire. This desire begins to dominate his mind, and when it is not reciprocated, it gives birth to anger—anger at himself, at her, at the world. His friends, who interact with her in a normal, casual way, cannot understand why he is so tormented. The answer is simple: it is not the girl who is the cause of his suffering but his attachment to her, his repeated belief that his happiness depends on her."

Guruji looked around the room, his gaze resting briefly on each devotee, as if drawing them into the story.

"This is how it begins for all of us," he said. "It starts with a simple stimulus—a sense object that catches our attention. This could be a person, a possession, or even a fleeting desire for recognition. The mind begins to contemplate it, and from this contemplation, attachment is born. Attachment leads to craving, and when that craving is thwarted, anger rises like a storm."

His tone grew more sombre as he explained the effects of anger. "Anger is not just an emotional reaction—it is a chain of destruction. First, it clouds our judgment, leading to delusion. Delusion bewilders our memory, causing us to forget what truly matters. And when memory fails, our intelligence—the very light that guides us—is lost. In this state, we fall into chaos, losing our sense of self and purpose."

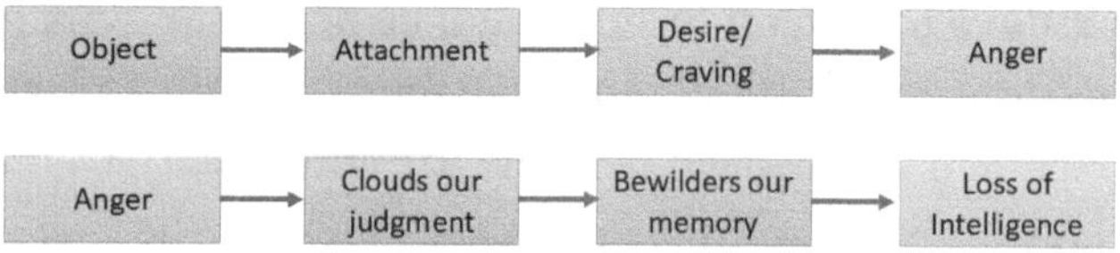

Guruji let the silence settle for a moment, allowing the gravity of his words to sink in. Then, his voice softened once more, offering a glimmer of hope. "But remember, anger is not your enemy. It is a messenger. It tells you where your attachments lie and where you need healing. To address it, you must begin at its root. Recognise the desires and attachments that fuel it. Cultivate detachment, not by rejecting the world, but by understanding that true fulfilment does not depend on external objects or circumstances."

He smiled gently, his eyes shining with the clarity of his wisdom. "Transform your anger into insight, just as a blacksmith tempers raw iron into a strong and useful tool. Let the fire of anger, when it arises, illuminate the parts of yourself that need attention and growth. And always remember: Awareness is your greatest weapon, and discipline is your strongest ally. When you master these, you are no longer the slave of anger—you become its master."

As Guruji's words settled over the hall like a balm, he said, "Remember this: Anger is not your enemy. It is a messenger, carrying the voice of your unspoken fears and unmet needs. Listen to it, learn from it, and let it guide you—not into destruction, but into deeper understanding."

Guruji, sensing the heaviness of the moment, smiled gently and said, "Let us walk through life not as warriors fighting anger but as alchemists, transforming its fire into light."

Aastha asked, "How does uncontrolled anger harm relationships and self-growth?"

Guruji's expression softened as he looked at Aastha. "Aastha," he said gently, "uncontrolled anger is like a wildfire. It begins with a single spark—a word spoken in haste, a slight, real or perceived—but once it catches, it spreads, engulfing everything in its path. The trees that took years to grow, the delicate ecosystems they supported, all reduced to ash in moments. Such is the power of anger when left unchecked—it destroys what is precious, both outside and within."

He paused, letting the analogy sink in, before continuing. "Relationships, Aastha, are like fragile threads woven into a tapestry. Each interaction adds a strand, and over time, a beautiful pattern emerges. But when anger is uncontrolled, it is like taking a sharp knife to that tapestry. A single outburst can sever threads that took years to weave. Words spoken in anger cannot be unsaid, and even if forgiveness is offered, the scar remains."

Guruji leaned forward, his voice tinged with sorrow but also with urgency. "Have you ever seen the ripples in a pond when a stone is thrown into it? The water doesn't just absorb the impact; the ripples spread outward, disturbing the surface far beyond where the stone landed. Anger is like that stone. Its effects are not limited to the moment of the outburst—it creates ripples that disturb the peace of relationships, sometimes for years."

labourGuruji said, "Let me narrate a story to illustrate his point. "There was once a young sculptor who worked tirelessly on a magnificent statue. Every detail, every curve of the marble, was a labor of love. One day, while carving the final detail, his chisel slipped, creating a small imperfection. Consumed by anger at his mistake, he struck the statue in frustration. The force of his blow cracked the entire piece, reducing months of effort to ruin. In his rage, he destroyed what he had spent so much time creating. Relationships are like that statue, Aastha. Built with care and effort, but fragile. A single moment of uncontrolled anger can undo years of trust and love."

Guruji's gaze moved across the room, resting briefly on each devotee. "But the harm of uncontrolled anger doesn't end with relationships," he continued. "It also poisons the self. Anger clouds our judgment and blocks our ability to introspect. It traps us in a cycle of blame and victimhood, where we fail to see our own role in the conflict. This prevents self-growth because growth requires awareness, humility, and the willingness to learn from our mistakes. When anger takes over, it is like a fog that obscures the path ahead, leaving us lost and directionless."

Guurji then shared a teaching from the Tao Te Ching. "The Tao says, 'The best fighter is never angry.' Why? Because anger blinds us to the bigger picture. It makes us reactive, not responsive. And when we react, we lose control—not only of the situation but of ourselves. A calm mind, on the other hand, can see clearly and act wisely, turning conflict into an opportunity for growth."

Guruji's voice softened as he offered a solution. "Aastha, the key to mastering anger lies in pausing before it consumes you. When you feel anger rising, take a moment to breathe. Ask yourself, 'What am I truly angry about? Is it the situation, or is it the expectations I placed on it?' Often, anger arises because reality does not align with our desires. By understanding this, you can begin to detach from the need to control everything and instead focus on what you can influence—your own response."

Guruji smiled gently, the warmth of his presence filling the room. "And remember, anger is not the enemy. Like fire, it has its purpose. When controlled, it can fuel your passion for justice, your courage to stand up for what is right, and your determination to protect what you love. But when uncontrolled, it consumes indiscriminately, leaving destruction in its wake. Learn to hold anger in your hand, not in your heart."

Guruji said, "Imagine a jar of water with sediment at the bottom. When shaken, the water becomes cloudy, and you can no longer see through it. This is what anger does to the mind. But if you let the jar sit still, the sediment settles, and the water becomes clear again. Similarly, when you pause, reflect, and breathe through your anger, clarity returns. Only then can you act in a way that heals rather than harms."

The hall was silent except for the faint rustling of the breeze outside. Aastha nodded, her eyes glistening with understanding. Guruji's words had reached a place deep within her, planting seeds of wisdom that would undoubtedly grow.

Abhirami asked, "Guruji, how can anger be channeled into productive energy?"

Guruji smiled gently at Abhirami's question. After a moment, he began, his voice a soothing balm that seemed to touch every soul present.

"Anger," Guruji said softly, "is not inherently destructive. Like fire, it is neither good nor bad—it simply exists. When uncontrolled, it burns and destroys. But when harnessed, it can illuminate, warm, and transform. The key, Abhirami, lies not in suppressing anger but in learning to channel it, to use its energy as a force for creation rather than destruction."

He paused, his gaze steady and compassionate. "Imagine a raging river," he continued. "If left unchecked, it floods the land, destroying homes and lives. But when we build dams and channels, that same river becomes a source of power, irrigating fields and generating electricity. Anger is like that river—a raw, powerful energy. When directed with intention, it becomes a catalyst for growth, change, and even justice."

Guruji leaned back slightly, his expression contemplative. "Let me share a story," he said. "There was once a young warrior named Arjun, filled with anger after witnessing the suffering of his people under a cruel king. His rage was a storm, threatening to consume him. But instead of letting it control him, Arjun sought the guidance of a wise sage. The sage said, 'Arjun, anger is your fire, but it must be tempered by wisdom. Let it fuel your purpose, not your destruction. Focus it like a beam of sunlight through a magnifying glass, and it will ignite not chaos, but change.' With the sage's guidance, Arjun transformed his anger into determination. He trained tirelessly, strategised meticulously, and eventually led his people to freedom—not with blind rage, but with focused resolve."

The devotees listened intently, their hearts stirred by the story. Guruji continued, "Anger, when suppressed, festers. It becomes resentment, poisoning the mind and body. However, when acknowledged and channelled, it becomes a source of strength. The Buddha, before enlightenment, faced the demons of desire, fear, and anger under the Bodhi tree. He didn't deny their existence—he observed them, understood them, and transformed their energy into compassion and wisdom."

Guruji leaned forward slightly, his voice gaining a subtle intensity. "Channelling anger begins with awareness, Abhirami. When anger arises, pause. Ask yourself, 'Why am I angry? What is the root of this emotion?' Often, anger stems from unmet expectations or perceived injustices. By understanding its source, you can redirect its energy toward constructive action."

Guruji's voice softened, carrying the weight of his next words. "Consider this: a sculptor wields a hammer and chisel to create beauty from stone. The same tools, if used in haste or rage, could shatter the stone. Your anger is the hammer. When wielded with awareness, it can shape your life and the world around you."

Guruji, after a pause, said, "Even in the Bible, anger is addressed with similar insight. In the book of **Ephesians 4:26-27**, we are told: *'Be angry, and do not sin: do not let the sun go down on your wrath, nor give place to the devil.'* This verse acknowledges that anger is a natural human emotion, but it warns against letting it fester, turning into a force of destruction. It emphasises the importance of channeling anger with restraint and wisdom, rather than allowing it to lead to harmful actions."

Guruji's eyes gleamed as he spoke, bringing the teachings into harmony. "In both the Gita and the Bible, the message is clear—anger is not the enemy. Rather, it is our relationship with anger that determines whether it becomes a destructive force or a tool for transformation. Krishna teaches Arjuna to act with purpose, and the Bible reminds us to resolve anger before it corrodes our soul."

To deepen the connection, Guruji recited a shloka from the Bhagavad Gita Chapter 5, Verse 26:

kama-krodha-viyuktaanam yatinam yata-chetasaam |
abhito brahma-nirvaanam vartate viditaatmanam ||

Meaning: "Those who are free from anger and desire, who have subdued the mind and know the Self, find peace everywhere and attain the bliss of Brahman."

Guruji paused to let the profound wisdom sink in. "The Bible encourages us to not let anger fester, and Krishna teaches us to free ourselves from its grip through self-mastery. Both guide us toward a path of liberation, where anger no longer controls us but becomes a tool for deeper understanding and action."

He smiled gently, concluding with a timeless insight. "Whether you look to the Gita or the Bible, the essence is the same: anger, when channelled with awareness and purpose, becomes a stepping stone to growth and righteousness. But when left unchecked, it becomes a snare that traps the soul."

Guruji's gaze swept across the room, his words resonating deeply. "Remember, anger can also be a teacher. It shows us where we feel powerless, where our boundaries have been crossed, or where our values are being threatened. By listening to what anger is telling you, you can align your actions with your highest self."

He then smiled a warm, reassuring smile that seemed to light up the entire hall. "But never forget, Abhirami, that anger must always be tempered by love and compassion. Without these, it becomes a storm that destroys indiscriminately. With them, it becomes a wind that clears the path ahead."

Guruji said, "Think of anger as the wind. A hurricane wreaks havoc, but a steady breeze propels a sailboat forward. When you learn to guide the wind of your anger, it can carry you toward your goals, rather than leaving destruction in its wake."

The room was silent, the devotees deep in thought. Abhirami's eyes shone with understanding, her question answered in a way that touched not just her mind but her soul. Guruji looked around, his voice now gentle but firm. "Channel your anger. Use it to build, to heal, to transform. Let it be a fire that warms, not a fire that burns."

Kiran asked, "Guruji, why is forgiveness essential in dissolving anger?"

"Forgiveness," Guruji began, his voice gentle yet powerful, "is not about excusing the wrongs of another or condoning their actions. It is about freeing yourself from the chains of anger that bind you to the pain inflicted by others. To hold onto anger is like grasping a burning coal with the intent of throwing it at someone else; in the process, you only scorch your hand."

He paused, allowing the analogy to resonate. "Kiran, anger and resentment are heavy burdens. They weigh down the heart, cloud the mind, and drain the soul. But forgiveness? Forgiveness is the act of releasing those burdens, of setting down the heavy load so that you can walk freely once more."

Guruji's voice softened as he began a story. "There was once a farmer who owned a small plot of land. One day, a neighboring farmer let his cattle stray into this land, trampling and ruining the crops. The first farmer was furious and vowed to get revenge. He spent days plotting, consumed by his anger, unable to focus on his other duties. His wife, seeing his turmoil, asked him a simple question: 'While you wait to hurt him back, who is suffering more—you or him?' Her words pierced his heart. He realised his anger had not brought him peace but had stolen it entirely. The next day, instead of revenge, he went to his neighbour and forgave him. To his surprise, the neighbor apologised profusely and promised to repay the damage. But more than the apology, what the farmer gained was his own peace."

Guruji looked around the hall, his gaze resting momentarily on each devotee as if to ensure they understood the weight of his words. "Anger is often justified in our minds. We cling to it, thinking it gives us power or control. But the truth is, anger controls us, not the other way around. Forgiveness, on the other hand, is an act of courage. It is a decision to break free from the cycle of pain and bitterness."

Guruji turned to Kiran, his tone deepening with emotion and reverence. "Kiran, forgiveness is a cornerstone of spiritual wisdom, a thread woven into the teachings of many faiths and philosophies. In the Bible, Jesus profoundly reminds us in *Matthew 6:14-15*: *'For if you forgive others their trespasses, your heavenly Father will also forgive you. But if you do not forgive others, neither will your Father forgive your trespasses.'* These words highlight a sacred truth—our willingness to forgive others mirrors our readiness to receive divine grace. Forgiveness, then, becomes more than an act of kindness; it becomes a path to divine alignment, a bridge between human imperfection and spiritual strength."

He paused, letting the weight of these words settle in the hearts of his listeners before continuing. "Similarly, in the Bhagavad Gita, Krishna speaks of forgiveness as an essential virtue of those who walk the path of divine wisdom. Chapter 16, Verses 1–3 illuminate the qualities of the divine nature, with forgiveness shining as a beacon of inner strength and grace:

shri-bhagavan uvacha
abhayam sattva-sanshuddhir jnaana-yoga-vyavasthitih
daanam damash cha yajnash cha svaadhyayas tapa arjavam
ahinsa satyam akrodhas tyaagah shantir apaishunam
daya bhuteshv aloluptvam mardavam hrir achaapalam
tejah kshamaa dhritih shaucham adroho nati-maanita
bhavanti sampadam daivim abhijatasya bhaarata
(*shri-bhagavan uvacha…*)

Meaning: 'O scion of Bharat, these are the saintly virtues of those endowed with a divine nature—fearlessness, purity of mind, steadfastness in spiritual knowledge, charity, control of the senses, sacrifice, study of the texts, austerity, and straightforwardness; non-violence, truthfulness, absence of anger, renunciation, peacefulness, restraint from fault-finding, compassion toward all beings, absence of covetousness, gentleness, modesty, and lack of fickleness, vigour, forgiveness, fortitude, cleanliness, freedom from malice, and absence of vanity.'

Krishna places forgiveness among the highest virtues, equating it to fortitude, purity, and compassion. It is not a passive act, Kiran; it is an active reclamation of your inner peace and strength. Forgiveness is the power to dissolve anger and bitterness, much like sunlight dissolves the morning mist, revealing the clarity and warmth beneath."

He leaned forward slightly, his voice steady yet imbued with deep compassion. "To forgive is not to forget the pain inflicted, but to release its grip on your soul. It is to choose peace over resentment, wisdom over reaction, and love over lingering hurt. Jesus and Krishna both teach us that forgiveness is not a sign of weakness; it is a profound demonstration of strength and spiritual maturity."

Guruji's eyes softened as he continued. "Imagine a tightly clenched fist. The longer you hold it, the more your muscles ache, and the more exhausted you become. Forgiveness is the act of releasing that fist, of letting go of the tension and pain. It is an act of self-liberation, not just a gift to the one who hurt you. When we forgive, we untie ourselves from the chains of anger and allow space for healing, growth, and divine grace."

He smiled gently, his gaze sweeping across the hall. "Forgiveness is not for the faint-hearted. It requires courage and humility. But when you embrace it, you will discover that it is one of the most liberating and transformative acts a human being can undertake. It cleanses the heart, uplifts the spirit, and aligns you with the higher truths that lead to eternal peace."

And yet, forgiveness is not always easy. It feels like giving up a part of ourselves, doesn't it? But think of a tree, Kiran. When its branches are broken by a storm, does it stop giving shade or fruit? No. It continues to give because that is its nature. Forgiveness is our nature, too, buried beneath the layers of ego and pride. When we forgive, we return to that divine essence within us."

Guruji's voice grew softer, but the impact of his words deepened. "Forgiveness is not a weakness; it is the ultimate strength. It takes more courage to let go than to hold on. When you forgive, you dissolve the anger that eats away at your soul. You create space for love, peace, and understanding to flourish. And in doing so, you not only heal yourself but also offer a chance for the other person to transform."

He smiled gently. "So, Kiran, when anger grips you, remember this: Forgiveness is not for the one who wronged you—it is for you. It is the balm that heals your wounds and sets you free."

The hall was silent, not with hesitation but with awe. Guruji's words had touched a chord, and the devotees could feel the transformative power of forgiveness taking root within their hearts. Kiran folded his hands in gratitude, his eyes brimming with understanding and a newfound resolve to practice forgiveness in his own life.

Guruji, after a long pause, spoke gently, his voice carrying a note of calmness and care. "Let us take a break for the mid-day meal." His words, though simple, felt like a blessing, a gentle reminder to nourish not just the spirit but the body, too.

The devotees slowly began to move out of Shambav Hall, their steps unhurried, as if still immersed in the profound energy of the morning session. Some chose to return to their resting quarters to refresh themselves, while others made their way to the food centre where the mid-day meal awaited.

The air was alive with the comforting aroma of South Indian cuisine—steaming rice, fragrant curries, tangy sambhar, and the unmistakable scent of freshly tempered spices. The clinking of steel plates harmonised with the soft hum of conversations as devotees settled at tables or formed small groups on the mats arranged neatly on the floor. Some had already started savouring their meals, their faces reflecting a quiet contentment.

Among the crowd, Akshaya, Padma, Vasudeva, and a few others discussed their plans for the break. They decided to gather near the majestic Banyan tree after the meal. The Banyan, with its ancient roots and sprawling canopy, had become a favourite spot for reflection and connection. Its shade seemed to hold the wisdom of ages, offering solace to those who sought it.

After half an hour, the group began to reassemble under the tree's vast embrace. Some devotees lay sprawled on the soft grass beneath its branches, their eyes closed in serene repose. Others strolled through the nearby gardens, where the vibrant colours of blooming flowers seemed to mirror the inner peace many felt. A few wandered further afield, enjoying the gentle rhythm of a long stroll, their minds still reflecting on Guruji's teachings from the morning.

Akshaya and the others sat in a small circle, their conversations a blend of introductions, shared experiences, and reflections. They laughed lightly, their voices mingling with the rustle of leaves overhead. Padma spoke of how the session had stirred something deep within her, while Vasudeva shared how he was beginning to see life from a new perspective. There was a sense of camaraderie growing among them, a bond forming in the shared journey of self-discovery.

Kiran, seated nearby, glanced at his watch and let out a soft sigh. "It's time for Guruji's session," he said, his tone laced with both anticipation and a hint of reluctance to break the tranquil spell of the moment.

The group rose slowly, brushing off the dust from their clothes and stretching briefly before making their way back to Shambav Hall. The sun, now slightly tilted in the sky, cast dappled patterns through the canopy of the Banyan tree, as if nature itself was preparing them for the wisdom yet to come. The air was filled with a quiet excitement, the kind that comes when hearts are open and ready to receive.

CHAPTER IV

The Enemy of Greed

"Greed whispers that the next possession, the next achievement, the next conquest will bring fulfillment. But like a mirage in the desert, each time we reach it, the thirst remains, and the chase begins again."

– Shree Shambav

Synopsis

This chapter delves into the destructive nature of greed (lobha) and its power to distort the mind and soul. Guruji explains that greed is born from a deep sense of lack—a yearning for more that blinds us to the abundance already present in life. Through engaging questions and profound teachings, Guruji illuminates how greed creates division within the self and among people, leading to isolation, dissatisfaction, and a never-ending cycle of craving.

He reveals the illusion behind ownership and material wealth, reminding us that true fulfillment cannot be hoarded or bought. The chapter concludes by exploring the transformative power of generosity as a path to liberation, where giving becomes a sacred act of dissolving ego and embracing interconnectedness. This section encourages readers to look beyond material possessions and recognize the richness of a heart free from the chains of greed.

Lobha - Attachment to Wealth and Power

Sam asked, "Guruji, why does greed make us feel perpetually unsatisfied?"

The scent of sandalwood lingered in the air, and a gentle breeze carried the soft rustling of leaves from the sacred banyan tree outside. Sam, his voice filled with curiosity and longing, leaned forward and asked, "Guruji, why does greed make us feel perpetually unsatisfied?"

Guruji remained silent for a moment, allowing the weight of the question to settle in the space around them. His eyes reflected both compassion and wisdom. Then, with a voice, he spoke.

"Greed is like drinking salt water," Guruji said. "The more you consume, the thirstier you become."

He paused, letting the metaphor sink in before continuing. "A mind consumed by greed is like a man lost in the desert, chasing mirages. Each time he reaches what he believes to be an oasis, it vanishes, and his thirst intensifies. Greed is never about the object of desire—it is about the emptiness within."

The Story of King Yayati:

Guruji's gaze swept across the hall as he began recounting an ancient tale. "In the Mahabharata, there is the story of King Yayati, who was cursed to old age but was given a unique opportunity—he could exchange his old age with someone else's youth. His son, Puru, out of love and duty, took on the burden, allowing Yayati to enjoy youth once more. But even after experiencing boundless pleasures, Yayati realised that no matter how much he indulged, his desires only grew stronger. In the end, he renounced everything and turned to a path of wisdom. He declared, 'Desire is never satiated by indulgence, just as fire is never extinguished by feeding it more fuel.'"

Guruji's voice softened. "Sam, do you see? Greed operates under an illusion—that fulfilment lies in acquisition. But in truth, every fulfilled desire only plants the seed for more. What was once a wish becomes a need, and what was once enough becomes inadequate. This is why those who chase material wealth, power, or status often find themselves feeling empty, restless, and perpetually unsatisfied."

The Roots of Greed: A False Sense of Lack

Guruji then turned toward the entire gathering and asked, "Where does greed arise from?"

A few devotees exchanged glances, uncertain of how to respond.

"Greed is born from a false belief that we are incomplete," he explained. "It stems from the illusion that something outside of us will fill the void within. But the moment we attain one desire, another takes its place, because the hunger was never for the thing itself—it was for a deeper fulfilment, a peace that cannot be found in possessions."

From the Bible Mark 8:36, Guruji quoted:

"For what shall it profit a man, if he shall gain the whole world, and lose his own soul?"

His words rang with truth. "Greed blinds us to what truly matters. It keeps us chasing endlessly, believing that happiness is always just one step away—one more achievement, one more possession, one more validation. But true peace is not found in accumulation. It is found in contentment, in the realisation that we already have everything we need within us."

Breaking Free from the Cycle of Greed

He leaned back and smiled gently. "Sam, if you feed greed, it grows. If you starve it, it withers. The secret to satisfaction is not in having more but in wanting less. The moment you recognise that you are already whole, that moment greed begins to dissolve."

Sofia asked, "Guruji, how does greed create division within and around us?"

The Chains of Greed: How It Divides Within and Without

Guruji's eyes reflected a quiet knowing, as if he had seen the ripples of greed fracture both hearts and worlds. He closed his eyes for a moment, allowing the weight of Sofia's question to settle in the stillness. Then, with the gravity of a river flowing through time, he began.

"Greed is like a knife with two edges—it does not just cut the world outside, but also wounds the self within. It creates a wall between what is and what we desire, between who we are and who we think we must become. It divides families, friends, and nations, yet its deepest wound is inflicted upon the soul itself."

He let the words linger before continuing. "Have you ever seen a spider weave its web? At first, it is a thing of beauty—intricate, delicate, strong. But the more the spider spins, the more it entangles itself, until it is trapped in its own creation. Such is the nature of greed. The more we crave, the more we spin illusions, believing that possession will bring completion. But instead of fulfilment, we create a prison of longing, isolating ourselves from true connection."

The Division Within

"Greed fractures us from the inside, setting up an endless war between contentment and craving. The Bhagavad Gita warns us:

dhyaayato vishayaan pumsah sangas teshupajaayate |
sangaat sanjayate kaamah kamat krodho 'bhijaayate | |

Meaning: "While contemplating the objects of the senses, one develops attachment to them. From attachment arises desire, and from desire, anger is born."

"When greed grips the mind, we live in perpetual dissatisfaction—never present, never at peace. We start seeing ourselves as 'not enough,' always in need of more wealth, more power, more validation. The heart becomes restless, torn between gratitude and insatiable hunger, between love and selfishness. And when greed is thwarted, it gives rise to jealousy, anger, and resentment, turning us against our inner wisdom."

The Division in the World

Guruji's voice grew softer, filled with both sorrow and compassion. "Greed is not content with staying within—it reaches outward, fragmenting relationships, societies, and civilisations. Families break over inheritance, friendships crumble over wealth, and entire nations go to war in the name of conquest. Greed whispers, 'There is not enough. Take more.' And in this taking, we divide the world into 'mine' and 'yours,' 'rich' and 'poor,' 'superior' and 'inferior.'"

"History is filled with rulers who sought to own everything, yet died with empty hands. The Roman emperors, who once commanded armies and hoarded treasures, are now only names in books. The kings who built golden palaces could not carry even a grain of gold beyond the grave. What remains of them? Only their deeds—whether they divided or united, whether they took or gave."

Guruji said, "Let me narrate a story: The mighty Alexander, who had once stood unchallenged on the battlefield, now lay motionless on his deathbed. His tent, usually filled with war plans and the echoes of triumphant celebrations, was now heavy with silence, broken only by the faint rustling of the wind and the hushed whispers of those standing by his side. His once-commanding voice had softened, and his once-mighty body, which had endured the weight of countless battles, now struggled to hold onto its last breath."

His **physician**, the one who had treated him through fevers and wounds, stood beside him with sorrow in his eyes. "Your Majesty," he said hesitantly, "I have done everything in my power. I have used the best medicines, the rarest herbs. But…" He swallowed hard, unable to finish his sentence.

Alexander smiled faintly as if amused by the irony. "So, even the greatest of physicians cannot hold back death," he murmured. "The gods have given their verdict."

His **minister**, a man who had guided his empire with wisdom, took a step forward. "Your Majesty, you have conquered the world. Nations trembled at your name. Is there anything left unfulfilled in your heart?"

A long silence followed. Alexander's eyes, once burning with ambition, now held a distant sadness. "Yes," he finally whispered, "there is."

He slowly turned his gaze to his **generals**, the warriors who had marched with him through storms and deserts, who had fought beside him in every battle. Summoning the last of his strength, he raised his hand and beckoned them closer. "My time has come," he said. "But before I leave this world, I have three wishes. And I command you to fulfil them without fail."

The men nodded, their expressions grave. "Speak, Majesty," one of them said.

The Three Final Wishes

Alexander took a deep breath, his voice barely above a whisper.

"First," he said, "I want my physicians to carry my body alone on the way to my grave."

The men exchanged confused glances. The physician, still standing by his side, looked stricken. "Majesty, why?"

"Because," Alexander said, "I want the world to see that no doctor, no healer—no matter how skilled—can prevent death when it arrives. Life is fragile, and no amount of medical knowledge can grant immortality. Let this be a lesson: do not take life for granted."

A solemn silence followed as the men absorbed his words.

"Second," Alexander continued, "I want the road to my grave to be strewn with gold, silver, and precious stones from my treasury."

This time, the minister could not contain his surprise. "Majesty, this is your wealth, your empire's riches. Why scatter it on the road?"

Alexander closed his eyes briefly. When he opened them, they held a deep regret. "So that people may see that wealth is meaningless in the face of death. I spent my entire life chasing power, hoarding treasures, building an empire. And now, not even a single coin will come with me. Let the world see that all our material possessions remain behind, and chasing them endlessly is a waste of a lifetime."

Tears welled in the minister's eyes, for he had seen the king's endless pursuit of conquest, his unquenchable thirst for more. And now, at the very end, Alexander had realised what truly mattered.

"And third," Alexander continued, his voice now faint, "let my hands dangle out of my coffin for all to see."

A gasp escaped one of the generals. "But Majesty… that is unheard of. Why do you wish this?"

A tired smile crossed the king's lips. "So that the world may witness the ultimate truth—that we come into this world empty-handed, and we leave empty-handed. No matter how much we conquer, how much we accumulate, we take nothing beyond the grave."

The Final Lesson

His words hung in the air like a heavy cloud, pressing into the hearts of those around him. The mighty Alexander, the one whom no enemy could defeat, had been conquered at last—not by man, but by time itself.

His **physician**, once full of hope, now stood powerless. His **minister**, once busy with the affairs of the empire, now saw the futility of it all. His **generals**, once eager for battle, now looked at their king with newfound reverence—not as a ruler, but as a mortal man who had finally seen the truth.

Alexander took one last look at his men—those who had followed him through blood and fire, through victories and defeats. Then, with a soft sigh, he whispered, "When you bury me, do not build a monument in my honour. Let my hands remain outside the coffin, so the world knows… even the one who won the whole world leaves with nothing."

With that, his eyes fluttered closed. A hush fell over the tent. The king who had roared in battle, who had commanded thousands, who had once dreamed of ruling lands beyond the ocean… had spoken his final words.

And in that moment, **Alexander the Great was no longer a conqueror—but a teacher**.

The Path Beyond Division

Guruji leaned forward, his eyes meeting Sofia's. "The antidote to greed is simple, yet profound: share. The more you give, the less greed can divide you from yourself or the world. In Jainism, the principle of

Aparigraha—non-possessiveness—teaches us that letting go of attachment frees the soul.

In Sufism, Rumi says, *'Be like a river in generosity, like the sun in compassion.'*

"When we shift from wanting to hoarding to wanting to give, we dismantle the walls of division. Instead of chasing wealth, we cultivate richness of heart. Instead of taking, we learn to serve. And in that, we find the unity that greed once sought to destroy."

He paused, letting the wisdom sink in. The hall was silent, but the devotees' hearts were stirred—some by the weight of truth, others by the whisper of a deeper realisation. Greed was not just an enemy outside; it was a shadow within. And only through self-awareness and generosity could they reclaim the light.

Alice's voice rose above the gentle rustling of leaves. "Guruji," she asked, her voice laced with curiosity and introspection, *"what is the illusion behind ownership and material wealth?"*

Guruji smiled softly and began his response with a story.

The Story of the Beggar and the King

"Once, there was a mighty king," Guruji began, "who ruled over a vast kingdom. His wealth was immeasurable—palaces adorned with gold, jewels that could blind the eyes with their brilliance, and granaries that never ran empty. Yet, despite possessing everything a man could dream of, the king was restless, forever seeking more. One day, he came across a beggar sitting beneath a tree, meditating with a peaceful smile on his face.

Curious, the king asked, 'Why do you seem so content? You have nothing—no home, no riches, no possessions to call your own. Yet, I, who have everything, am constantly anxious and unsatisfied.'

The beggar opened his eyes and chuckled. 'Oh, great king, you are mistaken. I have everything I need, while you, despite your treasures, are poor. You live under the illusion that you own your wealth, but in truth, your wealth owns you.'

The king frowned. 'What do you mean?'

The beggar picked up a handful of dust and let it slip through his fingers. 'The world is like this dust. It passes through our hands, yet we claim it as ours. You may hold it for a moment, but can you keep it forever?'

The king remained silent.

The beggar continued, 'One day, your wealth will belong to someone else. Your palaces will be occupied by another ruler. Even your name will fade into history. What you think you own is merely borrowed for a short while. The moment you realise this, you will find freedom.'"

Guruji paused, allowing the story to settle in the minds of the listeners. Then, he turned to Alice and continued.

The Temporary Nature of Possessions

"We live under the grand illusion that we own things—our wealth, our homes, even our relationships. But tell me, Alice, when you were a child, did you not hold a doll and claim it as your own, believing you would treasure it forever?"

Alice nodded slowly. "I did."

Guruji smiled. "And where is that doll now?"

She thought for a moment before answering, "Gone… either lost or given away."

"That is the nature of everything in life," Guruji said. "What we call ours is only ours for a fleeting moment. Just like the child who clings to a toy, believing it is the most precious thing in the world, we cling to our wealth, our possessions, our titles. But as time moves forward, what once seemed indispensable becomes insignificant."

He gestured toward the vast sky above them. "A bird builds a nest and calls it home, but the moment the seasons change, it flies away without a second thought. We, too, are travellers in this world, yet we foolishly believe we can own something permanently. The greatest kings have come and gone, yet none have carried their treasures beyond their final breath."

Lessons from Sacred Texts

"In the **Bhagavad Gita (2.71)**, Krishna tells Arjuna:

vihaaya kaaman yah sarvaan pumansh charati nihsprihah|
nirmamo nirahankaarah sa shaantim adhigachchhati||

'A person who has given up all desires for sense gratification, who lives free from cravings, who has given up all claims of ownership and is free from ego—such a person attains peace.'

This is the ultimate truth—peace is found not in possession but in detachment. The moment we let go of our desperate need to 'own,' we free ourselves from suffering."

Guruji then turned to the Bible for another perspective. "In **Matthew 6:19-21**, Jesus says:

'Do not store up for yourselves treasures on earth, where moths and rust destroy, and where thieves break in and steal. But store

up for yourselves treasures in heaven… For where your treasure is, there your heart will be also.'

Both Krishna and Jesus speak of the same truth. Material wealth is temporary. True wealth lies in wisdom, in love, in the peace that comes from knowing that nothing truly belongs to us."

The Mirage of Control

Guruji then drew an analogy. "Imagine walking through a desert and seeing a shimmering pool of water in the distance. Your throat is dry, your body is exhausted, and you are desperate for relief. You run toward it, only to find nothing. It was a mirage.

Material wealth is the same. It promises happiness, security, and fulfilment. But the moment you grasp it, you realise it was never real—it does not bring true peace. The more you chase, the more restless you become."

Alice's eyes widened as she absorbed his words. "So, Guruji, what should one truly seek?"

The Wealth That Cannot Be Taken Away

Guruji's expression softened. "Seek that which is permanent—love, wisdom, service, and truth. These are the only things that belong to you, for they are not bound by time.

Instead of hoarding wealth, share it. Instead of clinging to possessions, use them wisely. Instead of claiming ownership, become a steward. When you stop trying to possess the world, you realise that the entire universe is already yours."

The banyan tree rustled as a cool breeze swept through the courtyard, as if nature itself had bowed in agreement with Guruji's words. Alice sat in quiet contemplation, realising that she had spent much of her life chasing an illusion.

Guruji smiled, his voice barely above a whisper, yet carrying the weight of timeless truth. "Alice, let go of the illusion of ownership, and you will find true freedom."

Bhavya sat before Guruji, her voice tinged with curiosity and a quiet yearning. *"Guruji," she asked, "how can generosity serve as a path to liberation?"*

Guruji closed his eyes for a moment, letting the question settle in the air. Then, opening them with a deep gaze, he smiled gently.

The Story of the Two Rivers

"Bhavya," he began, "imagine two rivers flowing through the land. One river is wide, abundant, and ever-giving, nourishing the fields, filling the lakes, and quenching the thirst of all who come near. The other river, however, is afraid of loss. It hoards its waters, building up barriers to prevent anything from being taken. Over time, what happens? The first river thrives, its waters pure and replenished by the ever-flowing cycle of nature. The second river, however, stagnates. Its waters grow murky, and life begins to wither around it.

Generosity is like the first river. When you give freely, you remain in the flow of life, and what you give returns in unexpected ways. But when you hold on too tightly, fearing loss, you block the natural rhythm of existence—and suffering follows."

Bhavya nodded slowly, reflecting on the metaphor. Guruji continued, his voice like a river itself, flowing deeper into the essence of the teaching.

The Illusion of Loss and Gain

"The greatest fear people have," Guruji said, "is that giving will leave them with less. This is the illusion that binds us. But tell me, Bhavya, if you light a lamp and use it to ignite another, does your flame diminish?"

She shook her head. "No, Guruji, the light only spreads."

"Exactly," he said. "True wealth, true joy, true wisdom—these things multiply when shared. A miser may hoard his gold, but he is imprisoned by it, never tasting the freedom of generosity. A kind heart, however, gives without fear, and in doing so, experiences the boundless nature of existence."

Sacred Wisdom on Generosity

Guruji then turned to the **Bhagavad Gita Chapter 17 Verse 20**, where Krishna speaks of the highest form of giving:

daatavyam iti yad daanam diyate 'nupaakarine |
deshe kaale cha paatre cha tad danam saattvikam smritam ||

'Charity that is given without expectation, at the right place and time, to the deserving person—this is considered sattvic (pure) giving.'

He looked at Bhavya. "Krishna tells us that the purest form of giving is that which is done selflessly, without attachment to the outcome. This is the kind of generosity that liberates the soul."

Then, from the Bible, he quoted **Luke 6:38**:

'Give, and it shall be given to you; good measure, pressed down, and shaken together, and running over, shall men give into your bosom. For with the same measure that you mete with it shall be measured to you again.'

He smiled. "Jesus, too, speaks of the universal law—what we give returns to us in ways beyond measure. But only when we give with an open heart."

The Rich Man and the Saint

Guruji then said, "Let me narrate a story: There was once a rich man who had amassed great wealth, yet he lived in constant fear—fear of thieves, of losing his fortune, of never having enough. One day, he approached a wandering saint and said, 'O wise one, I have everything, yet I am miserable. Tell me, how can I find peace?'

The saint smiled and replied, 'Give away a portion of your wealth to those in need.'

The rich man was taken aback. 'But if I give, won't I lose?'

The saint laughed. 'On the contrary, you will gain something far greater.'

Skeptical but desperate for peace, the rich man reluctantly gave away a small part of his wealth. To his surprise, he felt a strange lightness in his heart. Encouraged, he gave more. Over time, his joy grew, and he finally understood—true wealth is not in what we keep but in what we share.

By giving, he had freed himself from the chains of greed, attachment, and fear. He had found liberation."

The Final Teaching: Giving as Liberation

Guruji turned to Bhavya, his gaze deep and unwavering. "Bhavya, when we hold tightly to what we have, we become prisoners of our own desires. But when we give—whether it is wealth, knowledge, kindness, or love—we break free from the illusion of ownership. We align ourselves with the vast, infinite nature of existence."

A gentle breeze stirred the leaves, as if nature itself whispered agreement. Bhavya, deeply moved, felt a shift within her heart.

Guruji said, his voice soft but filled with truth, "To give is to dissolve the self. To dissolve the self is to be free. And that is the path to liberation."

CHAPTER V

The Enemy of Attachment

"That which you hold onto most tightly is what holds you captive. Release your grip, and you will find that freedom was never outside—it was always within."

– Shree Shambav

Synopsis

Attachment (Moha) is the veil that clouds true perception, binding the heart to impermanent things and creating an illusion of ownership and control. It turns relationships into chains, possessions into burdens, and the self into a prisoner of fleeting desires. The deeper one clings, the greater the suffering when change inevitably arrives.

True love and attachment are often confused, yet they are opposites—one liberates, while the other ensnares. Love flows freely, embracing the ever-changing nature of existence, while attachment resists change, fearing loss. Understanding impermanence brings clarity, dissolving the illusions that cause fear, sorrow, and longing.

Detachment is not a rejection of life but an invitation to experience it more deeply. When there is no fear of loss, there is freedom to love without possession, to engage without entrapment, and to walk through life with open hands, embracing each moment as it comes. Only in letting go can true fulfillment be found.

Moha - Delusion, Clinging to the Impermanent

Aarna's voice was soft but carried the weight of a deep longing: **"Guruji, how does clinging to impermanent things lead to suffering?"**

Guruji closed his eyes for a moment as if listening to something beyond the present. Then, he began, his voice steady yet filled with emotion.

"Imagine a traveller lost in the desert," he said. "His throat is parched, his steps are heavy, and then, in the distance, he sees an oasis—cool water, lush trees, and shade. With all his strength, he runs towards it, only to find that it has vanished before his eyes. It was nothing but a mirage. Now, he is left not only with thirst but also with despair. This is the suffering of attachment—mistaking the impermanent for the eternal, hoping that which must change will remain unchanged."

Aarna listened intently as Guruji continued.

"All suffering begins with clinging," he said. "People hold on to youth, though the body ages with each breath. They hold on to relationships, though all bonds change over time. They hold on to wealth, though not a single coin follows them beyond death. They hold on to identity, though the self they were yesterday is not the self they are today."

He gestured towards the large Banyan tree. "Look at that tree. Its roots are deep, its branches wide, but even it will one day fall. If one were to weep for every leaf that falls, would life not be filled with endless sorrow?"

The Story of the Golden Bowl

After a pause, Guruji spoke again, this time with a tale.

"There was once a wise monk who possessed a golden bowl, a gift from his teacher. It was beautiful, finely crafted, and precious to him. One day, a storm came, and the bowl slipped from his hands, shattering on the ground. His disciple expected him to grieve, but the monk simply smiled. 'I saw this bowl as already broken,' he said. 'Every time I used it, I knew this moment would come. Because I accepted its impermanence, I cherished it more, and now that it is gone, I do not suffer.'"

Guruji's voice softened. "When you hold something as if it is already gone, you begin to love it without fear. You do not grip it in desperation. You do not suffer when it changes. This is the way to live with joy, free from the sorrow of attachment."

Lessons from the Bhagavad Gita

Aarna looked down, reflecting deeply. Guruji continued, now drawing from ancient wisdom.

"In the Bhagavad Gita Chapter 2, Verse 22, Krishna says:

vaasansi jirnaani yatha vihaaya
navaani grihnaati naro 'paraani
tathaa shariraani vihaaya jirnaanya
nyaani sanyaati navaani dehi

Meaning: "Just as a person casts off worn-out garments and puts on new ones, so too does the soul abandon a decayed body and enter a new one."

"This truth applies not only to the body but to all things in life. The house you live in, the people you love, even your own thoughts—all are ever-changing. Clinging to them as though they are eternal is the cause of suffering. But understanding their impermanence brings peace."

A gentle breeze rustled the leaves, as if nature itself was whispering agreement.

Freedom in Letting Go

"This does not mean we should not love, or care, or build," Guruji clarified. "It only means we should not become prisoners of what is bound to change. Love without clinging. Possess without attachment. Experience fully, knowing that all things will pass. This is true freedom."

Aarna smiled faintly, as if a burden had been lifted from her heart. She bowed to Guruji, who smiled in return.

"Like a river that does not mourn the passing of water, flow with life, knowing that everything is but a moment, here and gone. In that surrender, you will find peace."

"Guruji," he asked, his voice hesitant, *"what is the difference between love and attachment? Aren't they the same?"*

Guruji smiled, as if he had been waiting for this question. "Imagine," Guruji began, "a bird perched on your hand. If you love the bird, you will admire its beauty, care for it, and allow it to fly freely. But if you are attached to it, you will close your fingers around it, fearing it may leave. And in that grasp, the bird will struggle, suffocate, and perhaps even die. Love is open hands; attachment is a closed fist."

Dev listened intently, his thoughts stirring. Guruji continued, his voice carrying the weight of ancient wisdom.

The Story of King Bharata and the Fawn

"In the scriptures, there is a story of King Bharata, a noble ruler who renounced his throne to live in solitude and meditate upon the Divine. But one day, he rescued an orphaned fawn and began caring for it. His love for the deer turned into a deep attachment. Instead of meditating, he worried about the fawn's safety. He could not bear to be away from it, fearing it would be harmed. When death came for him, his final thoughts were not of Divine but of the deer. And so, in his next life, he was reborn as a deer himself."

Guruji's voice softened. "Attachment binds us. It keeps us trapped in cycles of longing and fear. But love—true love—frees both the lover and the beloved."

Dev looked down, contemplating his own relationships. "Guruji, does that mean we should not care deeply for others?"

Guruji shook his head. "No, my child. Love deeply, but do not cling. Love is like the sun, which gives warmth to all but demands nothing in return. Love is like the river, which nourishes everything in its path but never holds back its flow. Love is expansive, selfless, and liberating. Attachment, on the other hand, is possessive, selfish, and fearful."

The Wisdom of the Bhagavad Gita

Guruji quoted from the Bhagavad Gita Chapter 2 Verse 47):

karmany-evadhikaras te ma phaleshu kadachana |
ma karma-phala-hetur bhur ma te sango 'stvakarmani ||

Meaning: "You have the right to act, but not to claim the rewards of your actions. Let not the outcome bind you, nor let the fear of failure keep you from striving. Act with purpose, but without attachment—true mastery lies in effort, not expectation."

"This is the essence of love," he explained. "To give without expectation. To nurture without possession. To hold without imprisoning."

Love vs. Attachment in the Human Heart

Guruji continued, "Attachment asks, 'What can you give me?' Love asks, 'How can I serve you?' Attachment clings to the illusion of permanence, while love embraces the truth of impermanence. Love allows relationships to breathe, while attachment suffocates them with fear."

The Impermanence of All Things: The Key to True Freedom

John sat before Guruji, his brows furrowed in thought. "Guruji," he asked, his voice carrying the weight of deep contemplation, *"why is understanding impermanence essential for freedom?"*

Guruji smiled gently, as if John had unknowingly unlocked a doorway to one of life's greatest truths. He picked up a small clay pot beside him, holding it up to the light.

"This pot," Guruji began, "was once nothing but earth. A potter shaped it, gave it form, and now it holds water. But one day, it will crack, shatter, and return to dust. If one clings to the illusion that this pot will last forever, there is suffering. But if one understands that it was always destined to return to dust, there is peace. Life is no different."

John listened carefully as Guruji placed the pot down.

The Story of the Weeping Mother

"There is an old story," Guruji continued, "of a mother who came weeping to the Buddha, carrying the lifeless body of her only son. She pleaded, 'Lord, bring him back to life. I cannot bear this loss.'

The Buddha, in his infinite compassion, said, 'I will revive your son, but first, bring me a handful of mustard seeds from a household that has never known death.'

Hope filled the mother's heart. She went door to door, asking for mustard seeds, but each home she visited had its own story of loss—a parent, a child, a sibling. As she listened, she realised that death had touched every family, and that her suffering was not hers alone. She returned to the Buddha, tears flowing, and said, 'I now understand. No one is exempt from impermanence.' And with this acceptance, she found peace."

Guruji turned to John. "Suffering arises when we resist impermanence. We want our loved ones to stay forever, our youth to last, our achievements to remain untouched by time. But nothing in this world is permanent—not our bodies, not our possessions, not even the thoughts in our minds."

Guruji then quoted from the Bhagavad Gita Chapter 2 Verse 14:

matra-sparshas tu kaunteya shitoshna-sukha-duhkha-dah |
agamapayino 'nityas tans-titikshasva bharata | |

Meaning: "O son of Kunti, the non-permanent appearance of happiness and distress, and their disappearance in due course, are like the coming and going of winter and summer seasons. They arise from sense perception, and one must learn to tolerate them without being disturbed."

"This world is like the changing seasons," Guruji explained. "One moment, the sun shines brightly; the next, the storm clouds gather. If you believe the sunshine will last forever, you will suffer when it fades. But if you understand that both joy and sorrow come and go, you will remain unshaken."

The River and the Rock

Guruji said, "A rock fights against the river, resisting its flow, and so it is battered, worn down over time. But a leaf floats upon the water, moving with its current, without struggle, without fear. The wise one is like the leaf, flowing with life's changes instead of resisting them."

John felt something stir within him. He had spent much of his life trying to control things—his success, his relationships, his future. And yet, the more he tried to hold on, the more restless he became. He finally understood: Peace is not found in control but in surrender.

Guruji looked at him with deep kindness. "Impermanence is not a curse; it is the doorway to freedom. If nothing lasted forever, then pain, too, must pass. If all things are fleeting, then attachment is unnecessary. If you embrace impermanence, you will move through life with grace, unburdened by fear."

John nodded, his heart lighter than before. The fear of change no longer gripped him—it was replaced by a quiet understanding. He had found freedom.

The Paradox of Detachment: Embracing Life in Its Fullness

Nita bowed before Guruji and asked, "*Guruji, how does detachment deepen our ability to experience life fully?*"

Guruji's eyes gleamed with understanding, and a serene smile crossed his lips. He picked up a lotus from the brass bowl beside him and twirled it gently between his fingers.

"Look at this lotus, Nita. It grows in the mud, yet remains untouched by it. The water rolls off its petals without wetting them. This is detachment—not running away from the world, but remaining in it, experiencing it fully, without being bound by it."

Nita listened intently as the other devotees settled in, drawn to the profound silence before Guruji's words.

The Story of the Monk and the River

Guruji said, "Let me narrate a story: Once, a wise monk and his disciple were walking along a riverbank when they came across a woman struggling to cross. The monk, without hesitation, carried her across on his back and set her down safely on the other side. They continued their journey in silence. Hours passed, but the disciple's mind was restless.

Finally, he could contain himself no longer and asked, 'Master, we monks have taken vows never to touch a woman, yet you carried her on your back. How could you?'

The old monk smiled and replied, 'I put her down hours ago. Why are you still carrying her?'

This, Nita, is the essence of detachment. The monk helped, yet remained free of attachment to his action, while the disciple, though untouched, carried the burden of his thoughts. True detachment is not about renouncing the world; it is about releasing the mind from unnecessary burdens, so that life can be lived with lightness and clarity."

The Illusion of Possession

Guruji continued, "Many believe that attachment brings joy, but in reality, it brings suffering. Imagine holding a handful of sand. If you grip it tightly, it slips through your fingers. But if you hold it gently, it remains in your palm. This is how life works. Cling too tightly to relationships, possessions, or even your own identity, and you will suffer. But if you engage with the world freely, without clinging, you will experience it more deeply."

Guruji then quoted the Bhagavad Gita Chapter 2, Verse 47: *"You have the right to perform your duty, but never to the fruits of your actions. Let not the fruits of action be your motive, nor let your attachment be to inaction."*

"This is the key to experiencing life fully," Guruji explained. "If you work only for rewards, you will be forever anxious, fearful, or disappointed. But if you engage in life with complete presence, unattached to outcomes, you will be free. You will love without expectation, give without demand, and live without fear."

The Fire That Burns Without Smoke

Guruji said, "Imagine a fire that burns without smoke. It gives warmth and light, but does not suffocate. This is how the detached person moves through life—fully present, yet unburdened. They love deeply but do not possess, act with passion but do not crave results, and embrace change without resistance."

Nita's eyes glowed with understanding. "Guruji, so detachment is not about avoiding love, but about loving without chains?"

Guruji nodded. "Exactly. The more you let go, the more fully you can embrace life. To be attached is to fear loss, but to be detached is to trust the flow of life. In this trust, in this surrender, you will find true joy."

A deep silence filled the hall as Nita and the others absorbed Guruji's wisdom. The lotus in his hand remained untouched by the water—rooted in the world, yet free.

The Evening of Reflection

As the golden sun dipped beyond the horizon, the sky became a canvas of deep oranges and purples, painting the world with a quiet farewell. The day had been intense—filled with wisdom, deep contemplation, and the weight of truths that settled into the hearts of all who had gathered. Guruji, sensing the need for a pause, let his gaze sweep over the devotees and gently said, **"Let us take an evening break."**

The devotees slowly rose from their places, still lost in thought. Some wandered towards the refreshment centre, their voices carrying remnants of the session's teachings. Others found solace in steaming cups of coffee and chai, their fingers wrapping around the warmth as they exchanged quiet reflections.

The air was thick with the aroma of freshly brewed coffee mingling with the sweet, untamed scent of wildflowers carried by the evening breeze. Somewhere in the distance, a herd of cattle meandered back home, their bells chiming in rhythm with the fading light. Birds, their wings heavy from the day's flight, nestled into trees, filling the air with soft evening calls before surrendering to the night.

Some devotees chose to take a quiet stroll along the temple path, their footsteps slow and thoughtful. The cool wind wrapped around them, whispering secrets of the coming night. Shadows lengthened, and with them, a certain stillness embraced the space—not of emptiness, but of presence. The world itself seemed to pause.

Akshaya and the others, after their brief walk, felt the subtle pull of the Shambav Hall, as if wisdom itself was calling them back. The next session awaited, and with it, another journey into the depths of understanding. Without words, they turned towards the hall, their hearts open, their souls ready.

And so, beneath a sky where stars had begun to flicker awake, the seekers returned, not just to the hall—but to themselves.

CHAPTER VI

The Enemy of Pride

"Pride is the fog that clouds the mirror of truth. The more you cling to the image of yourself, the less you see who you truly are."

– Shree Shambav

Synopsis

Pride is a veil that blinds the mind and burdens the heart. It whispers illusions of superiority, making one forget the interconnectedness of all existence. When entangled in pride, one seeks validation, mistaking external approval for inner worth. This hunger for recognition strengthens the ego, creating a fortress that separates the self from the truth. True wisdom is found not in exalting the self but in dissolving the need for superiority. Humility is the antidote—it does not diminish one's value but reveals the vastness of what remains to be learned. Self-awareness becomes the light that breaks through arrogance, allowing one to see life through the lens of truth rather than self-importance. To walk the path of liberation, one must surrender the illusion of pride and embrace the wisdom of humility.

Mada - Ego, Arrogance, Self-Importance

The Illusion of Pride: A Barrier to True Self-Realisation

Lalitha, her voice tinged with curiosity and sincerity. *"Guruji, how does pride blind us to our true nature?" she asked.*

Guruji remained silent for a long moment, his eyes reflecting the weight of centuries of wisdom. Finally, he spoke, his voice calm. "Pride is a mask," he said, "one that covers not just the face but the soul. It is a fog that dims the light within, making a person believe they are separate, special, or superior. The greater the pride, the denser the fog, and the harder it becomes to see the truth."

He paused, looking at the devotees before him. "Let me tell you a story."

The Story of the King and the Hermit

Once, there was a mighty king who had conquered vast lands. His pride was as great as his empire, for he believed himself to be the wisest, the strongest, and the most powerful ruler to have ever lived.

One day, he heard of a hermit who was said to possess knowledge greater than any king or scholar. Intrigued but skeptical, the king visited the hermit's small hut deep in the forest.

The hermit welcomed him with a smile and offered him a cup of water. But as he poured, the cup overflowed, spilling water onto the ground.

"Why do you keep pouring when the cup is already full?" the king asked, annoyed.

The hermit looked at him and replied, "Because your mind is like this cup—full of pride. Until you empty it, no wisdom can enter."

The king was taken aback. "Do you mean to say I know nothing?"

The hermit smiled. "No, my king. I mean that as long as you think you already know everything, you will learn nothing."

The king, humbled, bowed before the hermit, realising for the first time that his pride had blinded him to the vastness of true wisdom.

The Nature of Pride and Its Consequences

Guruji continued, "Pride makes us believe we are more than we truly are. It builds walls between us and reality. Instead of seeking truth, we seek validation. Instead of embracing growth, we resist it. The greater the pride, the deeper the blindness."

Guruji then recited a verse from the Bhagavad Gita (16:4), where Krishna describes the qualities of those bound by illusion:

dambho darpo 'bhimaanash cha krodhah parushyam eva cha |
ajnaanam chabhijaatasya partha sampadam asurim | |

"Hypocrisy, arrogance, pride, anger, harshness, and ignorance—these belong to those with a demonic nature, O Arjuna."

Guruji looked at Lalitha. "Pride is not strength, but a weakness disguised as power. It prevents a person from seeing themselves clearly. It is the reason why a learned man may become a fool, while a humble seeker may become enlightened."

The Path to Liberation from Pride

"So, Guruji," Lalitha asked, "how do we free ourselves from this blindness?"

Guruji smiled. "The first step is awareness. Recognising pride is like waking from a dream. The second step is humility—not in words, but in the heart. A river does not lose itself when it meets the ocean; it becomes something greater. So too must we dissolve the false sense of self to merge with the infinite."

Guruji continued, "Do not mistake humility for weakness. It is the greatest strength. The bamboo bends with the wind and survives the storm, but the rigid tree falls. The wise man bows, while the ignorant stands tall in his illusion. True sight comes when the veil of pride is lifted."

Lalitha bowed deeply. "Thank you, Guruji. I now understand that pride is not a crown but a chain."

Guruji nodded, his eyes filled with kindness. "Break the chain, and you will see the truth."

The Hunger for Validation and the Illusion of Ego

Rohith asked a question that lingered in the hearts of many—why do we seek validation, and how does it feed the ego?

Guruji looked at Rohith warmly and said, "Validation is like a mirage in the desert. The more we chase it, the farther it moves away, leaving us perpetually thirsty. Why? Because the ego is never satisfied; it is a bottomless pit, always demanding more."

He picked up a clay lamp from the table, its flame flickering gently. "Tell me, Rohith, does this lamp seek approval for its light?"

Rohith shook his head. Guruji continued, "Yet, it burns steadily, offering warmth and guidance. A true being, like this lamp, does not need to be told that it shines—it simply does."

The gathering leaned in as Guruji's voice deepened. "From childhood, we are conditioned to believe that our worth is measured by the applause of others. A child is praised for walking, speaking, and achieving. Slowly, an unseen master is born within—the ego. This ego whispers, 'If they approve, you are valuable. If they don't, you are nothing.' It binds us to the opinions of others, making us prisoners in our minds."

A soft breeze stirred the room as Guruji continued, "Let me narrate a story of the sage and the traveller. A traveller once met a sage sitting by a river. Seeing the sage's tattered robes, the traveler laughed, 'You are just a poor man. What wisdom can you offer?' The sage smiled and replied, 'And who are you, traveller?' The man puffed his chest, 'I am a successful merchant, respected by many.' The sage dipped his hand into the river, lifted a handful of water, and let it slip through his fingers. 'Your respect,' he said, 'is like this water—impossible to hold. Today, they praise you; tomorrow, they forget you. If you define yourself by their words, you will always be a beggar of validation.'"

Guruji placed the lamp back on the table. "The world is fickle, Rohith. One moment, it lifts you high; the next, it abandons you. If you seek validation, you build your house on shifting sands. But if you seek truth, you stand on unshakable ground."

A hush settled over the gathering. Rohith lowered his gaze, understanding dawning in his heart.

Guruji concluded, "Let your worth be defined not by the approval of others but by the integrity of your soul.

When the need for validation fades, the ego dissolves, and what remains is freedom."

The Humility That Shatters the Illusions of Pride

Sujitha, her voice steady yet filled with curiosity, asked, "Guruji, how can humility help dissolve the illusions created by pride?"

Guruji smiled, his eyes holding the wisdom of countless ages. He picked up a brass bowl filled with water and gently tipped it, letting the water spill onto the earth. "Tell me, Sujitha, can this bowl hold more water if it is already full?"

She shook her head. "No, Guruji."

He nodded. "Pride is like a full bowl—it leaves no room for wisdom. It deceives us into believing we already know enough, that we are superior, and that we do not need to learn. But humility…" He lifted the empty bowl. "Humility is emptiness, a space that welcomes truth. Only when we empty ourselves of arrogance, can we receive the wisdom that life offers."

The disciples sat in rapt silence. Guruji's voice deepened as he continued, "Let me tell you a story."

The Emperor and the Beggar

"In a great kingdom, there once lived a mighty emperor known for his wealth and conquests. One day, as he walked through the marketplace, he saw a beggar sitting under a tree, smiling serenely. The emperor, puzzled, asked, 'Why do you smile? You own nothing.'

The beggar bowed and replied, 'Maharaj, I own something far greater than wealth—peace. And you, despite your riches, seem restless.'

The emperor scoffed. 'Peace? That is the illusion of the weak. Power is the true treasure of life.'

The beggar smiled again. 'Maharaj, may I show you something?'

Intrigued, the emperor followed him to the riverbank. The beggar picked up a handful of sand and held it tightly. The grains slipped through his fingers. Then, he held his palm open, and the remaining grains rested peacefully.

'Pride is a closed fist,' the beggar said, 'trying to hold onto everything, yet losing it all. Humility is an open palm, allowing what is meant to stay, to stay, and what is meant to leave, to leave.'

The emperor stood in stunned silence. He had spent his life conquering lands, but in that moment, he realised he had been conquered by his pride. He fell to his knees before the beggar and whispered, 'Teach me the way of humility.'"

Guruji's voice softened as he looked at Sujitha. "Pride creates the illusion that we are above others, that we must prove our worth through achievements and status. But humility dissolves this illusion, revealing that true greatness is not in how high we stand, but in how deeply we bow.

A tree laden with fruit bends low; a river that nourishes many flows in silence. The wise bow not because they are weak, but because they are strong enough to know that ego is the real weakness."

Sujitha's eyes glistened with understanding. She folded her hands in gratitude.

Guruji concluded, "Be like the open palm, not the clenched fist. In humility, there is freedom. In humility, there is truth."

The Light That Dispels the Shadows of Arrogance

Espen asked, "Guruji, how does self-awareness dismantle the barriers of arrogance?"

Guruji looked at Espen, his eyes deep with knowing, as if peering into the very core of human folly. "Arrogance is like a fortress built on a mountain of ignorance. The higher we build it, the further we isolate ourselves. We stand at the peak, looking down upon others, believing we are superior. But in truth, we are trapped. The walls that were meant to protect our pride become the barriers that imprison us."

Guruji, after a pause, said, "And what is the key to escape?"

Guruji smiled and said, "Self-awareness"

A hush fell over the devotees. Guruji continued, his voice carrying the weight of countless ages of wisdom.

"Imagine a man walking through the desert, convinced he is heading towards an oasis. His thirst is unbearable, his pride unwavering—he refuses to listen to those who tell him he is heading toward a mirage. His belief, his arrogance, blinds him to the truth. But the moment he stops, breathes, and questions his path, clarity arises. He begins to see beyond his illusion. This moment of realisation is self-awareness. It does not humiliate him; it liberates him."

A young student, intrigued, asked, "Guruji, how can we cultivate such self-awareness?"

Guruji smiled, as if waiting for the question all along. "Self-awareness begins where arrogance ends—at the doorstep of honest reflection. One must look into the mirror, not to admire, but to see oneself as one truly is. The Bhagavad Gita teaches in Chapter 6, Verse 5:

uddhared atmanatmanam natmanam avasadayet |
atmaiva hyatmano bandhur atmaiva ripur atmanah | |

Meaning: "*A person must elevate himself by his own mind and not degrade himself. The mind is a friend to the one who has mastered it, but an enemy to the one who is enslaved by it.*"

Arrogance is born when the mind becomes our enemy—when it clings to a false identity, believing itself to be superior. But self-awareness is the mind's friendship with truth. It is the ability to witness our thoughts, words, and actions without bias. When we see clearly, arrogance crumbles."

Espen nodded slowly, absorbing every word. Guruji's voice grew softer, yet more powerful.

"The river does not announce its greatness—it simply flows. The mountain does not demand reverence—it simply stands. The wise do not need validation—they simply exist in truth. The moment you awaken to your true nature, arrogance dissolves like mist before the rising sun."

A deep silence filled the hall, not of emptiness, but of reflection. Guruji closed his eyes for a moment, then whispered, "Self-awareness is not a battle against arrogance—it is the light that makes the darkness disappear."

CHAPTER VII

The Enemy of Jealousy

"Comparison is the mirror that distorts your own reflection—look too long into another's life, and you forget the beauty of your own."

– Shree Shambav

Synopsis

Jealousy is a silent poison that seeps into the heart, distorting perception and sowing seeds of restlessness. It arises from comparison, from measuring one's worth against another's, and from the illusion that fulfillment is a limited resource. This toxic emotion not only disturbs inner peace but also corrodes relationships, replacing joy with resentment. Jealousy thrives on insecurity—the belief that one is lacking, unworthy, or undeserving of life's abundance. Yet, in truth, every being has a unique journey, and no two destinies are meant to be the same. The antidote to jealousy lies in gratitude, in seeing abundance instead of scarcity, and in transforming comparison into inspiration. When one shifts focus from resentment to appreciation, from envy to self-growth, true freedom is found.

Matsarya - Envy, Comparison with Others

The Shadow of Comparison and the Poison of Envy

As the golden hues of dusk settled over the ashram, the devotees gathered once more in the tranquil embrace of the Shambav Hall. Astyn, her voice filled with both curiosity and hesitation, finally spoke.

"Guruji, why do we compare ourselves to others, and how does it lead to envy?"

Guruji looked at Astyn for a long moment, his eyes reflecting both compassion and knowing. He took a slow breath and began.

The Illusion of the Measuring Scale

"Comparison is a mirage—no matter how far you walk towards it, the water will always seem just beyond your reach."

From the moment we are born, we are conditioned to measure—who is taller, who is stronger, who is wealthier, who is more admired. Society whispers into our ears that worth is determined by how we stand against others, and so we step onto an invisible scale that never truly balances.

But what is this scale made of? It is built on illusion, on the false belief that one person's success means another's failure. A tree does not compare itself to another tree, nor does a river envy the ocean—it simply flows, fulfilling its own purpose. Yet, the human mind, trapped in its desires, constantly weighs itself against others, failing to see that every soul has its journey.

The Story of the Two Sculptors

There was once a king who summoned two sculptors to carve identical statues of Lord Vishnu for his grand temple. Both were given the same marble, the same tools, and the same time. The first sculptor focused only on his own work, chiselling with patience and devotion, lost in the beauty of his art. The second, however, kept glancing at the first—was he carving faster? Was his statue more detailed? Each time he looked, a seed of doubt and jealousy grew within him. His hands trembled, his focus wavered, and in his anxiety, he struck too hard—cracking the statue beyond repair.

When the time came to present the statues, the first sculptor's work was a masterpiece, while the second was left with only broken stone. The king sighed and said, *"The one who looked only at his own work created art; the one who kept looking at another created failure."*

This is the fate of those who compare—rather than perfecting their path, they become so consumed by another's journey that they lose their own.

Envy: The Fire That Consumes Its Own Vessel

"Envy is like drinking poison and hoping the other person falls ill."

Comparison is the mother of envy, and envy is the thief of joy. When we see someone having what we desire—be it wealth, success, love, or admiration—the mind whispers, *"Why them and not me?"* Instead of celebrating another's fortune, we allow jealousy to creep in, making us feel inadequate and resentful.

But the truth is, envy only harms the one who harbours it.

The Bhagavad Gita Chapter 16, Verse 21 speaks of the three gates to self-destruction—**kama (desire), krodha (anger), and lobha (greed).** Envy is woven from all three, leading only to restlessness and sorrow.

tri-vidham narakasyedam dvaram nashanam atmanah|
kamah krodhas tatha lobhas tasmad etat trayam tyajet||

Meaning: "There are three gates leading to the hell of self-destruction for the soul—lust, anger, and greed. Therefore, one should abandon all three."

Breaking Free from the Chains of Comparison

So how does one escape this endless cycle?

- **Recognise Your Unique Journey** – No two flowers bloom at the same time. You have your own path, your own purpose.

- **Turn Comparison into Inspiration** – Instead of envying another's success, learn from it. Let it ignite your own potential.

- **Practice Gratitude** – Shift your focus from what you lack to what you have. The mind cannot feel envy and gratitude at the same time—choose wisely.

- **Celebrate Others' Success** – What you bless, you invite into your life. When you celebrate others, you expand your own abundance.

Guruji's voice softened as he concluded:

"Imagine you are a traveller, walking on a vast path. Every person you meet is walking their own journey, some ahead, some behind, some taking different roads altogether. If you keep turning to look at them, you will trip over your own feet. But if you keep your eyes on your own path, you will walk with purpose, with grace, and with peace."

Astyn nodded, her heart lighter, as if a weight had been lifted. The devotees sat in deep silence, absorbing the wisdom, their minds no longer bound by the chains of comparison but freed by the clarity of their own journey.

Kieron asked, "Guruji, how does jealousy impact inner peace and relationships?"

"Jealousy," he began, "is like a drop of poison in a cup of clear water. It does not announce itself with force, nor does it shatter the cup—it simply spreads, silently corrupting the purity within. One sip, and it turns nourishment into suffering."

The devotees listened intently, the air filled with both curiosity and a quiet sense of introspection.

The Fire That Burns the Bearer

Guruji continued, "Jealousy is a fire that does not consume the object of envy but instead devours the one who carries it. It is an affliction that breeds in the mind, whispering, 'Why them and not me? Why do they have what I do not?' And the moment you entertain this voice, your peace begins to decay.

Imagine two friends who have walked together since childhood. One rises to great heights of success, while the other, despite working hard, struggles to achieve the same. Instead of feeling joy for the friend's success, envy creeps in, turning admiration into resentment. The bond that was once a source of strength becomes a silent battlefield of comparison. What once was love is now weighed down by unspoken bitterness. This is the nature of jealousy—it transforms blessings into burdens and distances hearts that were once close."

The Biblical Warning Against Jealousy

Guruji turned to the scriptures and spoke, "Proverbs 14:30 states, 'A tranquil heart gives life to the flesh, but envy makes the bones rot."

"Jealousy is not only an emotion—it is a silent disease. It eats away at the foundation of peace. A person consumed by jealousy does not live in the present; they are shackled to the illusion that another's gain is their loss. But in truth, success is not a limited well that runs dry when another drinks from it. When the heart is jealous, it does not see reality—it only sees a distorted reflection of fear and insecurity."

The Taoist Perspective: Flow Like Water

"In the Tao Te Ching, Laozi reminds us, *'When you realise nothing is lacking, the whole world belongs to you.'* The river does not envy the ocean, nor does the tree resent the mountain for its height. Each plays its role in the grand design. But human beings, bound by ego, compare their journey to another's, forgetting that every soul walks a unique path. When jealousy takes root, we resist the natural flow of life, and in that resistance, we suffer."

Guruji said, "Let me narrate a story: There were two merchants in a town, both successful in their own right. One of them, however, could not bear to see the other prosper. He constantly counted his neighbor's earnings, watched his trade, and measured his own joy by his competitor's failures. One night, he had a dream. An angel appeared and said, 'Ask for anything, and it shall be granted—but whatever you ask for, your rival shall receive double.'

The merchant thought deeply. If he asked for wealth, the other would have more. If he asked for wisdom, the other would be twice as wise. Unable to bear this thought, he finally said, 'Strike me blind in one eye.'

The next morning, he awoke with vision in only one eye, and he wept, not for his own loss, but because he knew his rival still had both."

Guruji sighed and looked at the devotees, "Such is the blindness of jealousy—it is not satisfied with one's own success, but rather with another's downfall. And in seeking another's ruin, we destroy ourselves first."

Overcoming Jealousy: The Path to Inner Peace

Akshaya asked, "Guruji, so how do we free ourselves from this burden?"

Guruji smiled and said, "The cure to jealousy is found in *gratitude and love."*

Instead of seeing another's success as a threat, view it as proof that the divine grants abundance freely. Instead of competing, celebrate. Instead of measuring yourself against others, walk your path with full awareness. Love is expansive, but jealousy is restrictive. The more you love, the more life flows effortlessly."

Guruji closed his eyes and recited a verse from the Bhagavad Gita (16.1-3):

shri-bhagavan uvacha
abhayam sattva-sanshuddhir jnaana-yoga-vyavasthitih
daanam damash cha yajnash cha svaadhyayas tapa arjavam
ahinsa satyam akrodhas tyaagah shantir apaishunam
daya bhuteshv aloluptvam mardavam hrir achaapalam
tejah kshamaa dhritih shaucham adroho nati-maanita
bhavanti sampadam daivim abhijatasya bhaarata
(*shri-bhagavan uvacha…*)
'O scion of Bharat, these are the saintly virtues of those endowed with a divine nature—fearlessness, purity of mind, steadfastness in spiritual knowledge, charity, control of the senses, sacrifice, study of the texts, austerity, and straightforwardness; non-violence, truthfulness, absence of anger, renunciation, peacefulness, restraint from fault-finding, compassion toward all beings, absence of covetousness, gentleness, modesty, and lack of fickleness, vigour, forgiveness, fortitude, cleanliness, freedom from malice, and absence of vanity.'

He then opened his eyes and softly said, "If your heart is filled with love, there is no space for jealousy. If you trust in the divine, there is no fear of lack. And if you celebrate others, you free yourself from suffering."

The hall was silent, not with emptiness, but with the weight of realisation. The devotees bowed their heads, contemplating the fire they had unknowingly carried within.

Abhilasha asked, "Guruji, what is the root cause of jealousy—lack or insecurity?"

The evening breeze whispered through the open hall as Guruji closed his eyes for a moment, letting silence settle before speaking. The devotees leaned in, sensing the depth of the question that had been asked.

Guruji opened his eyes, his gaze calm yet piercing. "Jealousy is not a single emotion—it is a chain that binds the mind to suffering. It is born from both lack and insecurity, yet it is neither lack nor insecurity alone. It is the illusion of separation."

The devotees sat in quiet contemplation as Guruji continued.

The Illusion of Lack: A Cup That Cannot Be Filled

"There was once a beggar who sat on an old wooden box outside a grand palace. Every day, he stretched out his hand, hoping for coins from passing strangers. One day, a wise traveller asked him, 'What is in that box?' The beggar shook his head, replying, 'Nothing, it is just an old box I have been sitting on for years.'

The traveller insisted he open it, and with great effort, the beggar pried it open—only to find gold and precious gems hidden within.

This," Guruji said, "is the reality of those who believe they lack something. They beg for what they already possess, blind to the abundance that lies within. Jealousy is born when we believe someone else has taken more from a world of limited resources. But true wealth—love, wisdom, inner peace—cannot be depleted. The sun does not shine less because another bask in its light. The river does not stop flowing because someone else has drunk from it."

The Fear of Insecurity: The Shadow That Follows

"But jealousy does not arise only from the illusion of lack—it is also rooted in insecurity. Insecurity is the shadow that follows doubt. It whispers, 'You are not enough. You will be left behind. You will lose what you have.'

A nobleman owned a magnificent jade cup known for its flawless beauty. He guarded it fiercely, fearing that someone would steal it. His fear grew so strong that he stopped drinking from it, then locked it away in a box.

Yet, his mind was never at peace. He saw every guest as a potential thief, every moment of joy as a threat to his possession.

One night, unable to bear it any longer, he buried the cup deep in the forest. The next day, he woke up tormented—what if someone found it? What if someone else now drank from it? The cup that had once brought him joy had now become the source of his greatest suffering.

This is the nature of insecurity—it makes us see loss even before it happens. We believe others threaten our place, our worth, our love. And in this fear, we imprison ourselves."

The Seeds of Jealousy

The wind stirred softly in the hall as Guruji's words echoed through the stillness. He let silence settle before continuing.

"To understand jealousy, one must return to the beginning—to the story of two brothers, Cain and Abel, where envy first cast its shadow upon the human heart."

The devotees sat in quiet anticipation as Guruji began to unfold the ancient tale.

The Two Offerings: A Moment of Divine Judgment

Cain and Abel were the sons of Adam and Eve, the firstborn of humankind. Cain, the elder, tilled the soil, coaxing life from the earth, while Abel, the younger, tended to the flocks, guiding his sheep through green pastures.

In time, both brought offerings to God. Cain placed before the altar the fruits of his harvest—grains, vegetables, the labour of his hands. Abel, too, made an offering, but he chose the best of his flock—the firstborn lamb, unblemished and pure.

And then, the moment of reckoning arrived. The fire of the heavens descended, consuming Abel's sacrifice, accepting it with divine favour. But Cain's offering remained untouched, unaccepted. A bitter silence filled the space between the brothers.

The Rise of Envy: A Wound in the Heart

Cain's heart burned. A storm of emotions raged within him—humiliation, anger, resentment. His mind whispered accusations: *Why him? Am I not worthy? Am I not the firstborn?*

But what had Abel taken from him? Nothing. His brother had merely given what was asked, yet Cain felt robbed—robbed of approval, of recognition, of worth.

God, seeing the unrest in Cain's heart, spoke to him gently:

"Why are you angry, Cain? Why is your face downcast? If you do what is right, will you not be accepted? But if you do not, sin crouches at your door; it desires to have you, but you must master it."

It was a warning, a chance for self-reflection. But jealousy does not listen—it only feeds upon itself.

The Choice: Growth or Destruction?

Cain could have asked himself: *Why was my offering not accepted? What can I do to improve?* But jealousy does not look inward—it looks outward, searching for someone to blame.

Instead of refining his heart, he let his resentment grow. He did not see Abel as a brother anymore, but as a rival, an obstacle, a shadow eclipsing his own light.

And so, in the fields where they had once played as children, Cain led Abel away. Under the open sky, where the sun shone upon their laughter, Cain struck his brother down. The earth, which had once nurtured their family, now drank Abel's blood.

The first murder. The first betrayal. The first victory of jealousy over love.

The Aftermath: The Price of Envy

When God asked Cain, *"Where is your brother Abel?"* Cain turned cold, his guilt hidden behind indifference.

"Am I my brother's keeper?"

But the earth cried out, bearing witness to the crime. And Cain was cast away, condemned to wander—a man who had lost everything, not because of Abel, but because of his own heart.

Jealousy is an Illusion

Guruji looked around at the devotees, his voice steady yet soft. *"Jealousy is a mirage. It makes us believe that another's success is our loss. That someone else's light dims our own. But the truth is, Abel never took anything from Cain. Cain's suffering came from his refusal to grow."*

"Jealousy is not about what others have—it is about what we refuse to see within ourselves. Instead of improving, we compare. Instead of growing, we resent. And in doing so, we destroy ourselves."

Guruji, after a pause, said, *So, when jealousy rises in you, remember Cain. Do not let envy master you. Instead, look within. Refine yourself. And know this: Another's success does not diminish your own—it simply means the light of the world has grown a little brighter."*

The Wisdom of the Tao: Flow Without Resistance

"In the *Tao Te Ching*, Laozi says:

'When you realize there is nothing lacking, the whole world belongs to you.'

A tree does not envy the sky, nor does the ocean compare itself to the land. Each exists as it is, without resistance. The Tao teaches us that everything flows in harmony when we stop grasping. But the jealous mind resists—it wants to hoard, to cling, to measure. And in doing so, it blocks the natural flow of abundance."

The Miser and the Moonlight

Guruji after a smile said, "Let me narrate a story: *A miser once built high walls around his house, fearing that others would steal from him. One night, he saw his neighbor bathing in the silver light of the moon. The miser sighed, realising that no wall, no gate, no lock could ever steal the moonlight away from another. He had spent his life hoarding what could not be hoarded, and in doing so, he had missed the joy of simply looking up at the sky."*

Guruji paused. "This is the wisdom that dissolves jealousy—understanding that what is meant for you will never miss you, and what is not meant for you cannot be held. Let others shine; their light does not steal from your own."

The Path Beyond Jealousy: Gratitude and Trust

"So how do we break free?" Guruji asked. "By replacing jealousy with gratitude. By trusting that, the divine gives each soul what it needs for its journey.

The bird does not envy the fish, nor does the sun compete with the stars. Each plays its role in the vast design of existence. The moment you recognise your purpose, jealousy dissolves. The moment you stop measuring, you start living."

He looked around the hall, his voice soft yet steady. *"Jealousy is not about lack. It is not about insecurity. It is about forgetting who you are."*

A deep silence followed as if the weight of the words had settled into the hearts of all who listened.

Akanksh sat forward, his eyes filled with both longing and curiosity. He spoke softly but with deep intent, "Guruji, how can gratitude and inspiration replace envy?"

Guruji closed his eyes for a moment, as if sifting through the wisdom of ages, then spoke, his voice calm yet resonant.

"Envy arises when we believe we are incomplete, when we measure our worth against another and find ourselves lacking. But tell me, is the river envious of the ocean? Does the moon compare itself to the sun?

Each has its own role, its own path. The river flows with devotion, carving valleys and nourishing the land. The ocean is vast, deep, and powerful in its stillness. Neither envies the other, for both exist in harmony with their nature."

A hush fell over the hall as Guruji continued.

Guruji's voice carried both weight and warmth as he spoke. "Consider the story of King Saul and David," he said. "Saul was once a mighty ruler, chosen and blessed by God. But when the people sang praises of David's victories—'Saul has slain his thousands, and David his tens of thousands'—his heart darkened with envy. Instead of recognising David as an ally, he saw him as a rival, a shadow threatening to eclipse his own light."

Guruji's gaze swept across the gathering, his voice steady yet poignant.

"What changed? Saul had not lost his kingdom, his power, or his anointing. Yet, jealousy poisoned his heart, turning admiration into resentment, trust into fear. He could have been a mentor, a guide—but instead, he let envy consume him. His downfall was not caused by David's success, but by his unwillingness to celebrate it."

Guruji paused, letting the gravity of the lesson sink in. Then, his tone softened, shifting to another perspective.

Guruji said, "Now, let us look at the opposite—John the Baptist. His disciples came to him, troubled that Jesus was gaining more recognition. But John, with deep wisdom and a heart free of jealousy, responded, 'He must increase, but I must decrease.' He did not see Jesus as a competitor but as a fulfillment. He knew his purpose was to prepare the way, not to claim the path for himself. His joy lay in serving, in uplifting another's light rather than fearing its brightness."

Guruji's eyes reflected quiet understanding as he continued, "This is the path of wisdom: to recognise that another's rise does not mean our fall. The light of one does not extinguish another, but together, they make the world shine brighter. Gratitude and inspiration, not envy, lead us to true fulfilment."

The devotees listened in silence, some nodding, others deep in thought. Guruji then said, "A seed that envies the towering tree forgets its own potential. A candle that envies the sun forgets the darkness it can dispel. When we turn envy into inspiration, we awaken to the truth: that another's greatness is a reminder of what is possible within us. Instead of saying, 'Why not me?' say, 'How can I learn?' Instead of feeling a lack, feel gratitude. Instead of resentment, cultivate admiration."

Guruji gestured toward the devotees.

"Gratitude is the antidote to envy. When you see the beauty in your own life, you stop yearning for another's. The Tao Te Ching teaches that 'contentment is the greatest wealth.' If we constantly chase what others have, we live in perpetual poverty, no matter how much we gain. But when we are grateful for what is, we realise we were never lacking to begin with."

Guruji's voice softened. "Let gratitude replace envy, and you will know peace. Let inspiration take its place, and you will know growth. When you admire someone, do not covet what they have—learn from them. Celebrate their success, and you will invite the same blessings into your life. This is the path of freedom."

A deep silence followed his words as if the universe itself had paused to listen. Some bowed their heads in contemplation; others closed their eyes, breathing in the truth. Akanksh, his heart lighter, smiled with understanding. The lesson was clear: Envy is a shadow, but gratitude and inspiration are light. And in choosing light, one finds liberation.

As Guruji closed his eyes, a deep silence filled the Shambav Hall. The energy of the day's session lingered in the air like the fading resonance of a temple bell. After a long pause, he slowly rose, his presence still heavy with the wisdom he had shared. With a gentle nod, he signalled the conclusion of the session and stepped out, leaving the hall in profound stillness.

The devotees followed, their hearts full yet contemplative. The night embraced them with a quiet, sacred beauty. The air was crisp and cool, carrying the faint scent of earth and wildflowers. Above them, the sky stretched vast and infinite, scattered with stars that shimmered like celestial lanterns. Wisps of clouds moved lazily across the heavens, veiling and unveiling the moon. The rhythmic hum of nocturnal birds mixed with the occasional chirp of crickets, and somewhere in the distance, the soft rustling of leaves whispered like an ancient hymn.

Some devotees made their way to the food centre, their conversations quiet, as if reluctant to break the spell of the evening. Others paused, gazing at the sky, absorbing the stillness before moving to refresh themselves.

Padma, Nita, and Lalitha stood near the entrance, their breaths visible in the cool air. "After dinner, let's meet at the fireplace," Padma suggested. The others nodded in agreement, sensing that the night still held space for reflection.

An hour later, they regrouped around the fire, its golden flames dancing against the dark backdrop of the night. The warmth of the fire wrapped around them, warding off the cold, its crackling sound merging with the hushed murmurs of their voices. They spoke of the day's session, unravelling its wisdom, each sharing their thoughts, doubts, and realisations.

Then, their conversation turned inward—toward themselves. One by one, they shared their journeys, their struggles, their silent battles. The fire bore witness to their vulnerabilities, its glow illuminating not just their faces but their souls. Some spoke of burdens they had carried for years; others reflected on lessons life had forced them to learn.

As the flames burned lower, their words grew softer, settling into silence. They sat there, simply being—letting the warmth of companionship and understanding fill the spaces where words were no longer needed.

One by one, they rose, returning to their resting places, the embers of the fire mirroring the quiet glow in their hearts. The night deepened, wrapping them in rest, while the universe above continued its silent, eternal watch.

.

PART THREE

The Final Battle

Beyond the Six Enemies

"The river does not doubt whether it will reach the ocean; it simply flows. The mountain does not question whether it stands tall; it simply is. Only the human mind, blessed with thought, is cursed with hesitation. Trust, and flow like the river."

-Shree Shambav

CHAPTER VIII

The Enemy of Fear

"Fear is not the walls around you but the ones within. You do not escape fear by running from it—you dissolve it by stepping beyond its illusion."

– Shree Shambav

Synopsis

Fear is the last and most insidious enemy that lurks within, binding the soul with invisible chains. It whispers doubts, fuels anxieties, and creates illusions of limitation. Unlike external enemies, fear is self-imposed—it thrives in the mind, distorting reality and preventing one from stepping into their true potential. While caution is a necessary guide, fear paralyzes, trapping individuals in cycles of hesitation and regret. The path to liberation lies not in eradicating fear but in transforming it—replacing uncertainty with trust, anxiety with awareness, and insecurity with the courage to embrace life fully.

Bhaya - Anxiety, Insecurity, Uncertainty

Before the Dawn – A Morning of Reflection

Before sunrise, Akshaya completed his morning rituals and meditation, stepping onto the rain-kissed pathway. The earth, damp from the night's downpour, carried the scent of fresh soil, and droplets still clung to the leaves, falling like pearls in the quiet morning air. Small rivulets, formed by the rain, meandered over the rocks, carving their own paths—an unspoken lesson in persistence and flow.

As he walked, the first notes of birdsong began to fill the air, delicate yet full of life. In the distance, he saw Vasudeva and Kiran approaching. Their presence blended seamlessly with the tranquillity of the morning.

Akshaya smiled and said, "The air is cool; the wind carries a freshness that awakens the spirit. It is a perfect morning for a stroll." The three of them walked together, their steps in rhythm with the stillness around them. Soon, others joined, drawn by the quiet harmony of the moment.

After a while, the scent of chai beckoned them, and they gathered for steaming cups of tea. Conversations flowed like the rivulets from the rain—light yet deep, carrying thoughts of the day's learnings and reflections.

Kiran, the ever-mindful timekeeper, glanced at the sky and gently reminded them, "Today's session begins earlier. We should prepare."

With that, they dispersed, each retreating to get ready, the morning's serenity still lingering in their minds.

The Gathering – A Question That Awakens the Soul

An hour later, the Shambav Hall brimmed with quiet anticipation. The devotees gathered, their hearts steady with devotion, their minds eager for wisdom. Guruji entered, his presence alone an anchor of peace. Taking his seat, he closed his eyes, drawing the room into a profound stillness.

The silence was not empty—it was full, alive, carrying the weight of centuries of seekers and saints who had asked the same questions, sought the same truths.

After a moment, Aastha spoke, her voice carrying both curiosity and longing.

"Guruji, how does fear restrict our potential and decision-making?"

The Cage of Fear and the Wings of Freedom

Guruji opened his eyes, his gaze deep as the ocean, reflecting lifetimes of wisdom.

"Fear is not merely an emotion," he began, his voice steady like the flow of an ancient river. "It is a force that builds walls where none exist. It whispers of danger even when there is none. It blinds the mind and chains the heart. Fear does not keep us safe—it keeps us small."

The hall fell into a deeper stillness. The question, now out in the open, had already begun unravelling its own answer.

The Elephant and the Rope

Guruji leaned forward, his eyes glimmering with a quiet intensity. "Have you ever seen an elephant in captivity? A creature of immense power, bound by nothing more than a thin rope around its foot. As a calf, it tried to break free but failed. Over time, it learned helplessness, believing that no matter how strong it became, escape was impossible. So, it never tries again. The rope is not what holds it back—its mind is."

He let the lesson sink in before continuing.

"So too does fear operate within us. We see a failure, a rejection, a loss in the past, and we allow it to define our future. We forget that we have grown, that our strength has increased, that we are no longer the child who once faltered. And so, we stay where we are, never testing the limits of our own potential."

Aastha shifted in her seat, deep in thought.

The Fear That Paralysed a King

Guruji then turned his gaze toward the fire lamp flickering in the hall. "Even the greatest have been shackled by fear. In the Mahabharata, Arjuna, the mighty warrior, stood on the battlefield of Kurukshetra, trembling with doubt. Fear clouded his mind—fear of failure, fear of dishonor, fear of hurting those he loved. He was ready to abandon everything, to turn away from his path. But Krishna, his divine charioteer, revealed to him a truth: 'Your fear is an illusion. Action driven by dharma can never lead to ruin. What binds you is not the battle outside, but the war within.'"

Guruji's voice softened as he added, "Once Arjuna saw beyond his fear, he was no longer paralysed. He fought, not with desperation, but with clarity, with purpose."

He paused, letting the moment breathe before asking, "How many of us stand at the edge of our own battlefield, refusing to move because we let fear speak louder than truth?"

Aastha lowered her gaze. The words resonated deeply, striking a truth she had long ignored.

Caution vs. Crippling Fear

Guruji then smiled gently. "Let me be clear: fear itself is not the enemy. Caution is necessary—when you walk near fire, you must respect its power. When you cross a river, you must know its depth. But there is a difference between wisdom and paralysis. Fear is crippling when it keeps you from ever stepping forward, from ever trusting that the current will not always sweep you away."

He took a deep breath, the quiet around him almost sacred.

The Wind and the Bird

Guruji said, "Let me narrate a story of a bird who feared the wind. She stayed in her nest, watching the trees sway, the clouds shift. 'The wind is too strong,' she thought. 'What if I fall? What if I am not strong enough?' So, she never left."

One day, a storm came, and her nest was torn from the tree. In that moment of crisis, she had no choice but to spread her wings. And what did she discover? That she had always been able to fly."

Guruji's voice softened. "Fear tells us to stay in the nest. But life will one day force us out. Wouldn't it be better to trust our wings before that day comes?"

Beyond Fear Lies Freedom

Looking into the eyes of his devotees, Guruji said, "Your potential is vast, limitless, waiting to be discovered. But fear will always try to convince you that the sky is small, that your wings are weak. Do not wait for the storm to teach you that you were meant to soar. Fly while the skies are clear."

Aastha let out a slow breath, her heart lighter than before. The lesson was clear: Fear was never meant to be a prison—it was meant to be a doorway. And beyond that doorway, freedom awaited.

The Role of Courage in Overcoming Fear

Breaking the silence, Kieron spoke, his voice steady yet contemplative.

"Guruji, what is the role of courage in overcoming fear?"

Guruji opened his eyes, the depth of countless lifetimes reflected within them. He took a slow breath and began.

The Fire That Melts the Chains

"Fear," Guruji said, "is like a chain forged not from steel, but from our own doubts, anxieties, and past wounds. We wear it unknowingly, mistaking it for protection, when in truth, it binds us, keeping us small, keeping us from the vastness of our own potential."

He looked around the hall, his gaze resting upon each soul before him.

"But courage," he continued, "is the fire that melts these chains. Courage is not the absence of fear—it is the willingness to walk forward despite it. It is the light that reveals the illusions we have mistaken for walls. It is the force that turns hesitation into movement."

The Warrior Who Found True Strength

Guruji's voice softened, yet its weight deepened as he continued.

"In a kingdom veiled by time, there lived a warrior whose name was spoken with awe. His sword had carved countless victories, his presence commanded respect, and his armor gleamed with the stories of battles won. But beneath the steel and the glory, fear clung to him like an unseen chain.

He feared failure—though he had never fallen. He feared loss—though he had never been defeated. And, most of all, he feared that no matter how many battles he won, he would never be enough.

One evening, as the sun bled into the horizon, an old sage arrived at the gates of the kingdom. The warrior, intrigued by the presence of one so frail yet unshaken, sought his wisdom.

The sage looked into the warrior's eyes and spoke, 'Draw your sword and strike me down.'

The warrior recoiled. 'I cannot,' he said.

The sage's voice remained steady. 'Why?'

'Because you are unarmed, and I do not strike the defenseless,' the warrior replied.

A slow smile crept across the sage's face. 'And yet, every day, you let fear strike you down. You see, fear is your true opponent, and it is unarmed. It has no sword, no shield—only the power you surrender to it.'

The warrior felt the weight of the words settle deep within him. His knees buckled, not from weakness, but from the realisation that all his battles had never been against the enemies before him, but against the doubts within him.

That night, he laid down his sword—not in surrender, but in understanding. He was not his victories. He was not his failures. He was something beyond both. And in that moment, he was free."

The Courage of Moses: Overcoming Fear with Faith

Guruji said, "The story of Moses's divine calling is one of the most profound narratives of fear, self-doubt, and ultimate surrender to a higher purpose. Found in **Exodus, Chapters 3 and 4**, it reveals how even the greatest leaders must first conquer the doubts within before they can change the world."

The Moment of Hesitation – Exodus 3:11-12

Moses, once a prince of Egypt, had spent decades in exile, living as a shepherd in Midian after fleeing Pharaoh's wrath. He was no longer the bold man who had once defended his people. Time had humbled him, and the weight of past failures clung to him.

Then, one fateful day, near **Mount Horeb**, he encountered the **burning bush**, a divine manifestation of God's presence. From the flames, God spoke:

"I am sending you to Pharaoh to bring My people, the Israelites, out of Egypt" *(Exodus 3:10)*

But instead of embracing this divine mission, Moses hesitated. Fear gripped his heart, and he responded:

"Who am I that I should go to Pharaoh and bring the Israelites out of Egypt?" *(Exodus 3:11)*

This question unveils deep insecurity. Moses was once royalty, raised in the halls of power, but now he was nothing more than a shepherd. He had no army, no authority, and no confidence—only the scars of past failure. He doubted his worthiness, his ability, and ultimately, his purpose.

But God did not reassure him by building up his personal strength. Instead, He said:

"I will be with you." *(Exodus 3:12)*

This is a profound truth: True courage is not found in self-reliance but in trust.

Moses' Continued Fear

Even after this divine assurance, Moses's fears did not subside. He voiced another doubt:

"What if they do not believe me or listen to me?" *(Exodus 4:1)*

Here, we see a universal fear—the fear of rejection.

Moses was not just afraid of failure; he feared being unheard, dismissed, and disregarded. He feared stepping forward only to be pushed back.

In response, God did not remove the challenge. Instead, He equipped Moses with miraculous signs—a staff turning into a serpent, a leprous hand healed, and water turning to blood—showing that divine power would work through him.

Yet still, Moses' heart wavered.

The Root of Fear – Exodus 4:10-12

Moses pleaded again, this time exposing the deepest source of his fear—his own inadequacy:

"Pardon your servant, Lord. I have never been eloquent, neither in the past nor since you have

spoken to your servant. I am slow of speech and tongue." *(Exodus 4:10)*

Moses focused not on God's strength but on his own weakness. How often do we do the same? How often do we let our own limitations define our destiny, rather than trusting in a power greater than ourselves?

But God's response was unwavering:

"Now go; I will help you speak and will teach you what to say." *(Exodus 4:12)*

Yet even then, Moses hesitated. Finally, God appointed Aaron, his brother, to speak on his behalf, but Moses was still the chosen leader.

The Insight: Courage is Trust, Not Strength

Guruji smiled and said, "Moses' story teaches us that fear does not disqualify us from our calling. Even those destined for greatness tremble before the unknown. But God did not remove the task from Moses—He simply reminded him who was truly in control."

Moses' courage did not come from erasing fear, but from surrendering it. This lesson is echoed across spiritual traditions:

- **Buddhist Sutras:** Fear arises from **attachment**—to certainty, to control, to the self. The Buddha taught that liberation comes **not from eliminating fear, but from understanding its illusion**.

The Path Beyond Fear

Guruji paused, his eyes steady, as if seeing beyond the walls of the hall into the hearts of his listeners. Then, he spoke:

- *"Fear is not a sign of weakness—even great leaders experience it.*
- *The path ahead is never about our own abilities but about trust in the presence that guides us.*
- *True courage is not the absence of fear but moving forward despite it."*

As silence settled in the hall, the devotees felt the weight of those words. Some lowered their eyes, reflecting on their own hesitations, their own fears.

Moses did not step forward because he became fearless. He stepped forward because he placed his trust in something greater than his fear.

In doing so, he changed history.

In the teachings of Zen, fear is likened to a cloud—impermanent, shifting, without substance. The way to overcome it is not to fight it, but to walk through it, knowing it will dissolve with each step forward."

The Courage to Step Beyond the Edge

Guruji looked upon his listeners, his voice steady as he said, "Courage is not the roar of a lion. It is the whisper that says, 'I will try again tomorrow.' It is the step taken even when the path is uncertain. It is the heart that chooses to love despite the risk of loss. It is the soul that trusts, even in the face of the unknown."

Fear tells us, 'Do not go beyond this point.' But courage replies, 'Step forward and see.'"

A deep silence followed, not empty, but full—full of realisation, full of quiet determination, full of the understanding that courage is not found in grand gestures, but in the smallest choice to move beyond fear.

The Thin Line Between Caution and Debilitating Fear

Astyn bowed with reverence before speaking. "Guruji, how can we distinguish between caution and debilitating fear?"

Guruji closed his eyes, letting the question settle into the stillness of the Shambav Hall. After a pause, he opened his eyes, deep and knowing, like the vast sky before a storm.

The Story of Two Travellers and the Storm

Guruji began: "Two travellers once set out on a long journey through the mountains. One was a wise elder, seasoned by many years of walking treacherous paths. The other was a young man, full of energy but burdened with doubt."

"As they approached a narrow cliffside trail, the young man froze. 'Master,' he whispered, 'this path is too dangerous. One wrong step and we will fall.'"

"The elder nodded. 'Yes, the path is steep, and the wind howls fiercely. But is it the danger you fear, or is it the thought of danger?'"

"The young man hesitated. 'I... I don't know. Should we turn back?'"

"The elder smiled. 'Watch and learn.' He bent low, testing the firmness of each step. He placed his staff carefully, ensuring balance before moving forward. He adjusted his posture to withstand the wind, then proceeded."

"'This,' he said, 'is caution. It is the wisdom of knowing risks and preparing for them.' Then he turned to the young man. 'Now, what would fear do?'"

"The young man looked down the path. 'Fear would tell me not to take a step at all. It would keep me frozen here, imagining the worst, or make me turn back before I even try.'"

"The elder nodded. 'Exactly. Fear distorts reality. It magnifies dangers beyond their true size. It whispers not of wisdom, but of paralysis.'"

Caution as Wisdom, Fear as Chains

Guruji looked around the hall, his voice steady like an ancient river.

"Caution is intelligence; fear is imprisonment. Caution sees reality clearly—fear sees only its own shadows."

Caution and fear may seem alike, but their essence is different:

- **Caution is awareness** – It teaches us to recognise danger and take necessary steps. It is why a bird inspects a branch before perching, why a wise man studies the river before crossing.

- **Fear is distortion** – It does not protect; it paralyses. It whispers endless "what ifs," keeping us from ever stepping forward.

Guruji said, "True mastery is not in endless striving, but in stillness. When you arrive at the state of non-action, you will find that nothing is left undone. The world does not yield to force; it unfolds for those who move in harmony with its rhythm."

He continued, "Fear binds us, making us cling desperately to illusions of control. But caution is wisdom—it is not resistance, but understanding. The river does not ask to be tamed; it simply flows. The wise do not fight against its current; they learn when to step in and when to let it carry them forward."

Moving Beyond Fear

Guruji's eyes lingered on each devotee. His words fell like gentle rain, seeping into thirsty hearts.

"When faced with a challenge, ask yourself: is this caution, or is it fear? Caution is the wise elder—it prepares, it adapts, it steps forward. Fear is the trembling youth—it sees only the storm, not the path through it."

"Caution is the wisdom of a bird who builds its nest away from predators. Fear is the bird who never dares to fly."

"Fear says, 'Do not go.' Caution says, 'Go carefully.' Fear makes the mountain seem taller than it is. Caution finds the best way to climb."

Then, Guruji smiled, a warmth in his gaze. "And so, when the path ahead looks uncertain, do not ask if it is safe. Ask instead—do I move forward with wisdom, or do I stand still because of fear?"

A hush settled over the hall. The devotees sat in quiet reflection, the lesson settling into their souls like a seed taking root.

The Bridge Between Fear and Faith

Sam bowed slightly, his voice carrying the weight of a question many carried in their hearts.

"Guruji, why is faith an antidote to fear?"

Guruji closed his eyes, breathing in deeply as if drawing wisdom from the very silence that surrounded them. After a long pause, he opened his eyes.

He spoke, his voice rich with knowing.

"Fear and faith are two sides of the same coin. Fear is the belief in the worst that has not yet happened; faith is the trust in something greater than ourselves, even when we cannot see the path ahead. One binds, the other liberates."

The Story of the Bridge in the Mist

Guruji said, "There was once a traveler who wished to cross a vast valley. A bridge was said to exist—strong, unwavering, built by the hands of wise men long ago. But as the traveller approached, the valley was covered in thick mist, obscuring everything. He could not see the bridge; only an abyss of uncertainty lay before him."

"His heart pounded. Doubts whispered, 'What if there is no bridge? What if it is broken? What if I fall?'"

"Yet, he had heard from many that the bridge was real. Those who had crossed before had spoken of its strength, of how it had carried them safely to the other side. But still, fear held him frozen at the edge."

"Finally, an old sage appeared and asked, 'Why do you hesitate?'"

"'Because I cannot see the bridge,' the traveller admitted."

"The sage smiled. 'And yet, it exists. Will you trust what others have walked upon, or will you stay here, trapped by your own doubt?'"

"The traveller took a breath, then stepped forward. With each step, the mist began to clear. The bridge had been there all along, waiting to be trusted. Faith did not change the bridge—it simply allowed the traveller to walk forward despite the unknown."

Faith Over Fear:

Guruji let the story settle before continuing.

"Fear is hesitation at the edge of the unknown. Faith is the courage to step forward even when the path is not visible. This truth echoes across all great teachings."

Moses and the Red Sea – Exodus 14:13-14, 21-22

"The Israelites stood at the edge of the Red Sea, with Pharaoh's army closing in behind them. Terror seized their hearts. 'Were there no graves in Egypt, that you have brought us to die in the wilderness?' they cried."

"Moses, filled with faith, declared: 'Do not be afraid. Stand firm, and you will see the deliverance the Lord will bring today." Exodus 14:13

"Then, the sea parted—not before they had faith, but after. The waters stood as walls, and the path appeared because they believed in the unseen."

"Had they given in to fear, they would have turned back to slavery. But faith became their bridge to freedom."

In **Exodus 14:13-14**, Moses reassures the Israelites, urging them to stand firm and witness God's salvation, declaring that their oppressors—the Egyptians—will soon be gone forever, for **"The Lord will fight for you; you need only to be still."**

Then, in **Exodus 14:21-22**, God parts the Red Sea with a powerful east wind, transforming it into dry land. The Israelites walked safely between towering walls of water, proving that faith in divine power can turn impossible barriers into pathways of deliverance.

Jesus and the Storm – Matthew 8:23-26

"One night, Jesus and his disciples were in a boat when a violent storm arose. The waves crashed, the wind howled, and fear took hold of them."

"Jesus, however, slept peacefully."

"The disciples, trembling, woke Him. 'Lord, save us! We are perishing!'"

"Jesus opened His eyes, looked at them, and asked, 'Why are you afraid, O you of little faith?' Then He stood, rebuked the winds and the sea, and there was great calm."

"Faith did not mean the storm would never come—but it meant knowing that the storm did not have the final power."

Arjuna on the Battlefield - Wisdom on Fear and Faith

Guruji's voice carried the weight of ages as he spoke.

"On the battlefield of Kurukshetra, Arjuna—the great warrior, undefeated in combat—stood paralysed. His hands trembled, his breath faltered, his mind clouded with doubt. He gazed upon the battlefield and saw not enemies, but teachers, relatives, and kin. His heart, once steadfast, wavered."

"He turned to Krishna, his divine charioteer, and said, 'I will not fight.'"

The silence after these words was heavy, as if the air itself understood the gravity of Arjuna's hesitation. Then, Guruji's voice, calm as a river yet deep as the ocean, continued.

"Arjuna was not merely afraid of death—he was afraid of consequence, of failure, of making an irreversible choice. His fear was not of war, but of what war would make of him."

Krishna, unmoved by Arjuna's turmoil, did not offer consolation. Instead, He spoke of a truth beyond fear, beyond death, beyond the fleeting turmoil of human existence. Guruji recited the sacred verses:

Bhagavad Gita 2:19-20 – The Eternal Nature of the Self

ya enam vetti hantaram yash chainam manyate hatam |
ubhau tau na vijanito nayam hanti na hanyate | |

Meaning: "Neither he who thinks the soul kills nor he who thinks the soul is killed truly understands. For the soul neither slays nor can be slain."

na jaayate mriyate va kadaachin
naayam bhutva bhavita va na bhuyah

ajo nityah shashvato 'yam puraano
na hanyate hanyamane sharire
Meaning: "The soul is never born, nor does it ever die. It has neither emerged into being, nor will it cease to exist. It is unborn, eternal, changeless, and ancient. It is not destroyed when the body is destroyed."

The Dream of Death – An Illusion Dispelled

Guruji paused and then spoke in a softer tone, letting the wisdom of these words settle.

"If we dream that our head is cut off, we feel pain, terror, suffering. We awaken, gasping, shaken by the horror of it. Yet, the moment we open our eyes, we realise it was only a dream—the pain was never real."

"In the same way, the illusion that we are this body binds us in fear. We fear suffering, loss, and death because we have not yet awakened to our true nature. But one who has awakened—one who knows they are the eternal soul—has no fear of death, for they know they were never truly born and can never truly perish."

Faith in the Eternal vs. Fear of the Fleeting

"Arjuna's fear was not cowardice—it was attachment. He saw life through the lens of the temporary. Krishna did not dismiss his emotions but lifted his gaze beyond them."

"Fear sees only this battle, this loss, this fleeting moment of suffering. Faith sees beyond—to the eternal, to the unchanging, to the truth that no sword can cut, no fire can burn, no time can erode."

Guruji looked into the eyes of his devotee, his voice firm yet filled with compassion.

"When we are trapped in illusion, fear is inevitable. When we awaken to truth, faith becomes our only reality. And in faith, fear dissolves, like mist before the morning sun."

Guruji referred to **Tao Te Ching, Chapter 76**, where Lao Tzu teaches:

"When alive, man is soft and supple; in death, he becomes stiff and rigid.
The hard and unyielding belong to death;
The soft and flexible belong to life."

Guruji continued, "Rigidity is resistance, and resistance leads to suffering. The tree that refuses to bend in the storm is the first to break, while the reed that sways with the wind endures. True strength lies not in hardness, but in adaptability, in flowing with life rather than fighting against it."

Guruji, after a pause, said, "What does this mean? Fear resists, clings, stiffens against the unknown. Faith surrenders, flows, and adapts like water. Water does not fear the rock—it moves around it, wears it down, transforms it over time."

"Thus, faith is not blind—it is the deepest intelligence, the willingness to trust the currents of existence rather than fight against them."

The Light in the Darkness

Guruji looked into Sam's eyes.

"Sam, fear is not the enemy. It is the doorway. But you must decide: will you stand at its threshold, trembling, or will you walk through it?"

"Fear says, 'What if I fall?' Faith says, 'What if I fly?'"

"Fear sees only the night; faith trusts that dawn will come."

"Fear asks for guarantees; faith moves even without them."

Then Guruji smiled, his voice like a warm breeze at the break of dawn.

"You do not need to erase fear. You only need a faith greater than it. The bridge is already there—you simply have to walk it."

Sam bowed his head as did the others, their hearts lighter, their burdens less heavy. The wind whispered through the trees outside, carrying with it the echo of truth:

Fear may whisper, but faith moves mountains.

The Sacred Pause: A Moment Between Wisdom

As the session took a pause, the devotees stepped outside into the embrace of the morning—a world freshly bathed in the night's rain. The air was crisp, carrying the scent of damp earth and the lingering fragrance of wild flowers. The sun, still veiled behind the swaying branches, cast golden streaks through the leaves, as if nature herself were waking from deep meditation.

The rhythmic croaking of frogs filled the silence, a song of gratitude for the rains that had quenched the earth. Crickets whispered their quiet melodies, blending into the rustling leaves, while birds, stirred by the rising light, broke into song—some calling out in joyful anticipation, others merely murmuring drowsily, savouring the last moments of dawn's tranquillity.

With steaming cups of aromatic chai and strong coffee, the devotees found solace in this interlude. The tea carried the essence of spice and warmth, the coffee a bold, awakening depth—each sip a reminder of life's simple pleasures. Butter biscuits, crisp and golden, crumbled in their mouths, dissolving into a sweetness that lingered like unspoken words of gratitude.

Some devotees sat in quiet reflection, their eyes lost in the horizon, as if searching beyond what was seen. Others engaged in hushed discussions, unravelling the layers of Guruji's wisdom, their words weaving through the morning air like sacred verses. A few laughed, exchanging lighthearted moments, their mirth blending with the whisper of the wind—because wisdom, too, must be balanced with joy.

As time passed, the golden hues of morning deepened. The devotees, sensing the hour, set aside their cups and conversations. One by one, they made their way back to Shambav Hall, their steps steady, their hearts open, ready for the next lesson. The pause had not been mere rest—it had been an immersion, a communion with the rhythm of existence itself.

And now, with spirits renewed, they gathered once more before Guruji, awaiting the next drop of wisdom to ripple through their souls.

CHAPTER IX

The Enemy of Doubt

"Doubt is like a shadow—it grows when we turn away from the light. Walk towards the light of faith, and the shadow will shrink behind you."

– Shree Shambav

Synopsis

Doubt is a silent enemy that erodes confidence, delays decisions, and traps us in a cycle of hesitation. It makes us question our abilities, our purpose, and even the universe itself. Doubt arises from past failures, fear of the unknown, and attachment to certainty. But what if doubt is not meant to paralyse us, but to be a bridge toward deeper faith?

This chapter explores how doubt can be transformed into wisdom, how faith is not blind belief but a cultivated trust in the flow of life, and how we can integrate logic and intuition to move forward. The greatest leaders, thinkers, and spiritual figures faced doubt—yet they did not remain in its grip. True strength comes not from never doubting but from learning to rise beyond it.

Sanshaya - Lack of Trust in Oneself and the Path

The Chains of Doubt and the Bridge of Faith

Espen asked, "Guruji, how does doubt keep us stuck in indecision and fear?"

As Espen's voice echoed through the hall, a silence settled among the devotees. The question was simple, yet profound—one that had haunted countless seekers across ages. Guruji closed his eyes for a moment, as if reaching beyond time, and then began to speak.

The Parable of the Two Travellers

Guruji said, "Once, two travellers set out to cross a vast desert. One carried a map, the other carried doubt. The first looked at the map, saw the marked paths, and walked forward with steady steps. The second, however, examined the same map but hesitated. *What if this path leads to danger? What if the guide who made this map was mistaken? What if I am not strong enough to cross the desert?* And so, while the first traveller moved ahead, the second remained stuck, paralysed by his own uncertainty."

Guruji's gaze swept across the hall. "Doubt is not the absence of truth—it is the refusal to trust it. The traveller who doubted did not lack the ability to cross; he lacked the belief that he could."

The Root of Doubt – A Mind Divided

"Doubt is not an enemy in itself. It is like a locked door—it can either trap you inside or push you to seek the key. The problem arises when we let doubt linger too long, turning it into fear. Fear of making the wrong choice, fear of failure, fear of the unknown. And when fear takes hold, action ceases. Indecision becomes a prison."

He paused, then continued.

"Tao Te Ching: *'Do you have the patience to wait till your mud settles and the water is clear? Can you remain unmoving till the right action arises by itself?'* True wisdom is not found in endless questioning but in allowing clarity to emerge."

Walking on Water

Guruji looked at Espen. "In the Bible: Matthew 14:28-31, Peter experienced this very struggle. When Jesus walked on water, Peter, filled with faith, stepped out of the boat. For a moment, he, too, walked upon the waves. But then, doubt crept in. He saw the storm, the winds, and he began to sink."

Guruji's voice softened. "Jesus did not scold Peter for sinking—He asked, *'Why did you doubt?'* Peter's failure was not in his action but in his hesitation. The same waters that carried him in faith consumed him in doubt."

The Sword of Wisdom – Cutting Through Uncertainty

"So how do we break free from doubt?" Guruji asked. "By realising that certainty is never external—it is an inner state. The warrior does not wait until all danger has passed before drawing his sword. He acts, knowing that wisdom is forged in movement, not in waiting."

The Bridge of Faith

Guruji's voice resonated with warmth. "Doubt will always exist, just as the mist clings to the morning hills. But the sun always rises, burning away the fog. Your mind may question, but your heart must walk forward. Take a step—not because you have no doubt, but because you have the courage to walk despite it."

A deep silence filled the room as his words settled. Espen bowed his head, the weight of hesitation slowly lifting from his shoulders.

The Bridge of Trust and the Abyss of Doubt

Bhavya bowed slightly before speaking, her voice carrying a quiet sincerity.

"Guruji, why is trust in oneself essential for progress?"

"Imagine," he began, "a traveller standing before a vast chasm. On the other side lies his destination—his dreams, his purpose, his true self. A narrow bridge stretches across the abyss, swaying in the wind. This bridge is trust. If he steps forward with faith in himself, the bridge holds firm. But if doubt takes root, his steps falter, and the chasm below becomes his reality."

He looked around at the assembled devotees. "This is the journey of every seeker. Without trust in oneself, progress is impossible. Doubt is the weight that keeps our feet nailed to the ground."

The Story of the Bamboo and the Oak

Guruji said, "Let me narrate a story of two trees that stood side by side—a mighty oak and a humble bamboo."

"One day, a great storm came. The oak, confident in its strength, stood rigid, resisting the wind. But as the storm raged on, its mighty branches began to crack. Unable to bend, the oak finally split and fell.

The bamboo, however, trusted in its nature. It bent with the wind, yielding but never breaking. And when the storm passed, it stood tall once more."

Guruji smiled. "This is the power of self-trust. When we trust ourselves, we become like bamboo—adaptable and unbreakable. But when we doubt ourselves, we become rigid, like the oak, vulnerable to life's storms."

Guruji said, "He who lacks trust in himself finds the world reflecting his doubt, for trust given is trust returned."

"Trust is a cycle. If we do not trust ourselves, we project that doubt onto the world, and in return, the world does not trust us. But when we trust our path, the universe bends in our favour."

The Bhagavad Gita – Arjuna's Doubt

Krishna tells Arjuna **Bhagavad Gita Chapter 4, Verse 40)**:

ajnash chaashraddadhanash cha sanshayatma vinashyati |
nayam loko 'sti na paro na sukham sanshayaatmanah | |

Meaning: "But those who lack both faith and wisdom, consumed by doubt, are bound to falter. The skeptical soul finds no peace—neither in this world nor beyond."

"Arjuna, the greatest warrior of his time, stood paralysed on the battlefield—not by enemy swords, but by his own mind. His doubt blinded him. Krishna reminded him that self-trust is the foundation of action, of dharma, of life itself."

Trust: The Foundation of All Progress

Guruji gazed at Bhavya, his eyes filled with warmth. "When you doubt yourself, you hesitate. When you hesitate, you do not act. And when you do not act, you remain stagnant.

Self-trust is not arrogance; it is the quiet knowing that you are capable, that you are guided, that you are enough.

The journey is long, the storms will come, and the bridge will sway—but if you trust yourself, your feet will never fail you."

The Dance of Reason and Faith: Aarna's Question

Aarna sat with a contemplative gaze, her voice carrying both curiosity and uncertainty.

"Guruji, how can we balance reason with faith in overcoming doubt?"

Guruji closed his eyes for a moment, as if listening to something beyond words. Then, he opened them and smiled gently.

The Two Wings of a Bird

"Reason and faith are like the two wings of a bird," he began. "A bird cannot fly with just one wing. If it has only reason, it remains grounded, forever analysing, forever questioning, never taking the leap. If it has only faith, it may soar for a time but will struggle to navigate, blind to the winds that shift around it. True flight comes when both are in harmony."

He paused, allowing the imagery to settle, then continued.

The Story of the Lost Navigator

"There was once a skilled navigator, a man of the sea, who prided himself on his knowledge of the stars, the winds, and the currents. He believed in logic, in calculation, in the science of direction. But one day, a mighty storm arose, shrouding the sky and rendering his instruments useless.

In desperation, he turned to an old fisherman on the boat, a man who had sailed these waters for decades.

'How do we find our way?' the navigator asked.

The old man simply closed his eyes, inhaled deeply, and said, 'Trust the sea, listen to the wind.'

The navigator scoffed. 'That is foolishness! Without my charts, my compass, how can I trust the sea?'

The old fisherman smiled. 'Because the sea has never left us. It has always carried us home—when we remember how to listen.'

That night, with no tools but his instincts and the wisdom of the fisherman, the navigator guided the ship safely to shore. And in that moment, he understood: logic gave him knowledge, but faith gave him direction."

The Flow of Trust

Guruji paused, his eyes reflecting the depth of ancient wisdom. Then, in a voice as gentle as flowing water yet firm as the earth, he said:

"He who clings too tightly to intellect becomes rigid, like a tree that snaps in the storm.
He who drifts blindly in the unseen becomes lost, like a ship without a compass.
True wisdom flows like water—deep in understanding, yet free in trust."

The river does not stop to question each rock in its path, nor does it force its way blindly. It moves with both awareness and surrender, knowing it will reach the ocean."

The Path Forward: Balancing Faith and Reason

Guruji looked at Aarna, his voice now filled with a quiet power.

"Reason helps us understand the world, but faith helps us move forward despite uncertainty. When reason and faith walk hand in hand, doubt loses its grip.

When the navigator used his instruments, he was wise. But when the storm rendered them useless, he had to surrender to something deeper.

When Peter walked on water, his faith lifted him. But when he let reason alone dictate his reality, he sank.

When you question, use reason. But when you must act, trust."

He smiled and concluded, "Use reason to light the lamp, but let faith be the flame that carries you through the darkness."

Aarna bowed her head, her heart a little lighter, her doubts a little softer. The dance between reason and faith had just begun.

The Light That Dispels the Fog of Uncertainty

Vidyarthi bowed and asked, "Guruji, how does clarity of purpose dissolve uncertainty?"

Guruji closed his eyes for a moment, letting silence settle over the hall like the morning mist before dawn. When he opened them, his gaze held the weight of countless truths.

"Uncertainty is like a dense fog," he began. "When the path is unclear, every step is hesitant, every movement riddled with doubt. But purpose is like the sun—when it rises, the fog dissolves, and the road ahead is revealed."

The Archer Without a Target

"There was once a young archer who wished to master his skill. He trained daily, yet his arrows often missed their mark. Frustrated, he sought out a wise master.

The master gave him a bow and arrow and took him deep into the forest. They stopped in an open clearing.

'Shoot,' the master instructed.

The archer looked around, confused. 'At what?'

The master smiled. 'Exactly. If you have no target, where will you aim?'

The young man understood. He had practiced endlessly, but without a clear purpose, his efforts were scattered.

When we do not define our purpose, every decision feels uncertain, and doubt thrives in the absence of direction."

Flow Without Resistance: The Wisdom of the River

With a gentle smile, he spoke.

"Imagine a river," he began, his voice as steady as the current of a great stream. "Born from the melting snow high in the mountains, it begins as a small, uncertain trickle. Yet, as it moves, it grows. It does not hesitate, nor does it question the path before it. It flows, trusting the pull of gravity, the silent call of the ocean."

The devotees listened intently, drawn in by the imagery.

"Along its journey, the river meets obstacles—sharp rocks, steep cliffs, dry land. But does it stop? No. It moves around the boulders, carves through the mountains, reshapes the very landscape that sought to contain it. Not with force, but with persistence. Not with resistance, but with surrender. And so, it reaches its destination—not because it fought the journey, but because it embraced it."

Guruji paused, letting the weight of his words settle.

The Man Who Fought the Current

Guruji said, "Let me narrate a story. Once, there was a man who lived by the river. He was strong, determined, and full of will. One day, he set out in a boat, rowing upstream with all his might. The current pushed against him, relentless and unmoved. But he refused to yield. His arms burned, his breath became laboured, yet he pushed forward, convinced that strength alone would lead him where he wanted to go.

Days passed, and his progress was slow. Weary and exhausted, he finally collapsed in his boat. And at that moment, he let go of the oars.

The river embraced him, carrying him effortlessly downstream. He realised then that all his struggles had been unnecessary. Had he trusted the current from the beginning, he would have moved forward with ease."

Guruji's eyes twinkled as he looked at his students.

"Many of us live like that man—resisting life, forcing our way, exhausting ourselves with unnecessary struggle. But wisdom is learning to flow, to trust that life has a rhythm far greater than our fears and doubts. The river does not fight, yet it moves mountains."

The Clarity Within

His voice softened, carrying the weight of deep truth.

"Clarity of purpose is not something we search for outside—it is revealed when we quiet the mind. The river does not stand still, waiting for certainty before it moves. It surrenders, and in that surrender, it finds its way.

Doubt arises when we forget who we are and why we are here. But when we awaken to our deeper truth, uncertainty dissolves like mist before the morning sun.

When we stop fighting life and begin to trust its flow, we move forward—not with struggle, but with grace."

Vidyarthi sat in silence, his heart lighter. He bowed deeply, understanding now that the path ahead was never meant to be forced—it was always there, waiting to be embraced.

The Weight of the Unforgiven Soul

Sofia asked, "Guruji, how does self-forgiveness free us from the chains of the past?"

Guruji looked at Sofia, his eyes deep with understanding. He let a silence settle before speaking.

"Imagine a traveller," he said, "walking a long road with a heavy sack of stones upon his back. Each stone represents a past mistake, a regret, an unhealed wound. As he walks, the burden grows heavier, his steps slower. Others pass him by with ease, but he struggles, weighed down by something invisible yet crushing.

Now, what if I told you—the sack was never tied to him? That at any moment, he could set it down and walk freely? This is the power of self-forgiveness. We imprison ourselves with guilt long after the world has moved on. We clutch our mistakes like chains, believing that suffering is the only way to redemption."

He paused, allowing the words to sink in.

The Prodigal Son: A Return to Grace

In the Bible, Jesus tells the parable of the Prodigal Son (Luke 15:11-32), a powerful lesson on forgiveness and grace.

A young man, eager for freedom, asks his father for his inheritance while his father is still alive—a request that, in those times, was as good as declaring his father dead in his heart. With wealth in hand, he leaves home, chasing pleasure and indulgence. But soon, his fortune runs dry, and famine strikes the land. Desperate and starving, he finds himself tending pigs—considered one of the most degrading jobs in his culture.

At his lowest, he realises his mistake. **But he does not return home with hope—only with guilt.** He believes he has lost his worth, that he no longer deserves to be called a son. Instead, he prepares himself to beg his father for a place as a mere servant.

But then something remarkable happens.

When his father sees him from a distance, he does not wait. He runs to his son, embraces him, and welcomes him home. There is no punishment, no scolding, no demand for repayment—only love. He calls for the finest robe, a ring, and a feast, rejoicing that his lost son has returned.

This is the nature of true forgiveness. The son was ready to carry the burden of guilt for the rest of his life, but his father had already forgiven him. His suffering was not because he was unwelcome—it was because he had convinced himself that he no longer belonged.

Guilt is like wandering in a far-off land, believing we are unworthy of returning home.

Self-forgiveness is the moment we realise: we were never exiled—only lost.

When we finally let go of guilt, we do not just return to love—we realise it was waiting for us all along.

Buddha and the Empty Cup

Guruji took a deep breath and continued.

"When Buddha was once asked about forgiveness, he picked up a cup of tea and said, 'If this cup is full of poison, how can I fill it with nectar?' The student replied, 'By emptying it first.'

'Yes,' Buddha said, 'and so it is with the heart. A heart full of self-hatred cannot receive peace. First, you must pour out your suffering.'

When we refuse to forgive ourselves, we hold onto poison, expecting it to nourish us. But poison does not heal—it only prolongs the suffering. The moment we choose self-forgiveness, we make space for grace."

The Ocean and the River

Guruji smiled at the gathering. "Think of a river flowing toward the ocean. No matter how polluted the river has become, the moment it merges with the vastness of the ocean, all impurity dissolves.

In the same way, when we surrender our guilt to self-forgiveness, we merge with something greater—love, wisdom, and renewal. We become free."

Sofia's eyes welled with tears. She understood now—she had been carrying a burden she never needed to bear. The past could not be undone, but the future was hers to embrace.

The Weight of Guilt and the Light of Awareness

Dev asked, "Guruji, what is the difference between guilt and healthy self-awareness?"

"Guilt is like a heavy chain," Guruji began, his voice steady. "It binds us to the past, trapping us in endless self-condemnation. It whispers, 'You are unworthy. You are beyond redemption.' But healthy self-awareness is different—it is a mirror, not a chain. It allows us to see our mistakes clearly, to understand them without being consumed by them. One drowns us; the other guides us forward."

Judas and Peter: The Two Paths of Guilt

"In the Bible, we see two men who faltered—Judas Iscariot and Peter. Both betrayed their Master. Judas, for thirty silver coins, and Peter by denying Jesus three times.

Judas was overcome by guilt. He saw his mistake, but instead of seeking redemption, he let his shame consume him. He believed there was no way forward and took his own life.

Peter, too, was devastated by his actions. But rather than let guilt define him, he turned to repentance. He wept, but he also walked forward, using his failure as a lesson rather than a life sentence. He became one of the greatest teachers of faith, proving that a moment of weakness does not have to define a lifetime.

The difference? Judas carried guilt like a stone that sank him. Peter carried awareness like a torch that lit his path."

The Uncarved Block and the Cracked Pot

Guruji said, "The **uncarved block**—a state of being pure and whole, unburdened by self-judgment. When we carry guilt, we take a chisel to that block, carving away at ourselves, believing we must punish ourselves into shape. But self-awareness does not destroy the block—it polishes it, bringing out its natural beauty."

Guruji smiled and said, "A man carried two pots every day to fetch water. One pot was whole, the other cracked. The cracked pot felt shame, believing it was worthless, spilling water along the way. One day, the man showed it the path it had watered—flowers blooming where its leaks had nourished the earth.

'You thought you were failing,' he told the pot, 'but you were giving life.'

Mistakes, when met with self-awareness instead of guilt, become the very things that help us grow. Guilt sees only failure; awareness sees the lesson."

The Mirror and the Chain

Guruji's voice softened. "When you look at yourself, Dev, do you see a prisoner weighed down by regret, or do you see a traveller who has learned from the road behind him?

Guilt is the voice that says, 'You have fallen, and you can never rise again.'

Self-awareness is the voice that says, 'You have fallen; now, stand up and walk forward.'

One is a prison. The other is a path. The choice is yours."

Dev sat still, as if seeing himself for the first time—not as a man chained by his past, but as a seeker holding a torch, ready to move forward.

The Alchemy of Guilt: Turning Burden into Light

Rohith asked, "Guruji, how can we transform guilt into personal growth?"

Rohith's question lingered in the air like the last note of a distant bell. The hall was silent, yet the question had stirred something in many hearts. Guilt—who had not felt its weight? Who had not been haunted by the echoes of their past missteps? Guruji closed his eyes for a moment, and then he spoke.

The Blacksmith and the Fire

"Imagine a blacksmith," Guruji said, his voice steady and deep. "He holds a piece of iron in his hand—rough, cold, and unshaped. If he keeps it as it is, it remains useless. But when he places it into fire, something remarkable happens. The heat softens it, makes it malleable, and with each strike of his hammer, it takes form—a sword, a tool, something of purpose.

Now, think of guilt as that piece of iron. Left untouched, it remains a cold burden in our hearts, weighing us down with regret. But when we place it in the fire of self-awareness, it softens. When we strike it with reflection and action, it transforms—not into suffering, but into wisdom."

Guruji let his words settle before continuing.

David's Fall and Rise: From Guilt to Purpose

"In the Bible, the story of King David is a powerful testament to transformation. Though he was a man after God's own heart, he faltered—he took what was not his, committed grievous sins, and carried the crushing weight of guilt. Faced with his wrongdoing, he could have allowed shame to consume him, sinking into despair. But instead of letting his past define him, David chose to learn from it. He wept in sincere repentance, sought redemption, and emerged with greater wisdom. Through humility and a renewed sense of purpose, he led with deeper compassion. His mistakes were not erased, but they became stepping stones to his transformation. His story reminds us that true redemption is not about forgetting the past—it is about using it to shape a better future."

Guruji paused and looked at Rohith.

"This is the secret: **guilt is not meant to be a life sentence—it is meant to be a teacher**. The greatest among us are not those who never fail, but those who take their failures and turn them into stepping stones."

The River and the Rock

Guruji said, "Water is the essence of resilience—fluid, soft, and yielding. Yet, over time, it carves canyons through mountains, shaping the very earth that resists it. The rigid may appear strong, but it is the adaptable that endures.

A river does not stop when a boulder obstructs its course. It does not sit in despair, asking, 'Why must this obstacle be here?' It does not curse the stone, nor does it turn back. Instead, it moves—finding a way around, flowing over, or seeping through the cracks, embracing the path that unfolds before it. The river does not fight resistance; it lets resistance shape it.

Guilt is the boulder in our way. If we stand before it, trapped in regret, we remain stagnant. But if we learn from it, if we let it guide us toward wisdom, if we shift our course instead of halting our flow, we become like the river—ever-moving, ever-growing, and ultimately, unstoppable."

The Garden of Growth

"Imagine two people," Guruji continued. "Both make the same mistake. One buries himself in regret, letting guilt consume him like weeds overtaking a garden. The other looks at his mistake, learns from it, and changes—he pulls the weeds, plants new seeds, and allows his garden to flourish.

Both had guilt. But only one transformed it into growth."

The Final Lesson

Guruji's eyes softened. "The past does not exist to torment us—it exists to teach us. If you carry guilt, do not let it break you. Let it shape you. Take responsibility, make amends if needed, and move forward with a heart that is wiser, stronger, and kinder.

Your mistakes are not meant to define you. **They are meant to refine you.**"

Rohith sat still, feeling something shift within him. The weight in his heart was still there, but it no longer felt like a chain. It felt like something else—like iron in the hands of a blacksmith, waiting to be forged into something greater.

CHAPTER X

The Enemy of Guilt

"To carry guilt forever is to chain yourself to a moment that no longer exists. True growth comes when you forgive yourself enough to become who you were meant to be."

– Shree Shambav

Synopsis

Guilt is a shadow that lingers long after the mistake has passed. It whispers that one is unworthy, undeserving of forgiveness and binds the soul to the past. But is guilt a punishment, or can it serve a greater purpose?

This chapter explores the nature of guilt and its impact on spiritual and emotional well-being. It reveals how guilt differs from self-awareness, how it can be transformed into growth rather than suffering, and how self-forgiveness is the key to breaking free from its chains. True healing comes not from clinging to guilt but from using mistakes as stepping stones toward wisdom.

Through reflection, stories, and insight, it becomes clear that guilt is not meant to imprison—it is meant to awaken.

Paap Bodh - Self-Punishment for the Past

The Weight of Yesterday

Alice asked, "Guruji, why do we hold onto guilt, even after learning from our mistakes?"

Guruji looked at Alice, his gaze steady yet filled with warmth. He closed his eyes for a moment, as if feeling the weight of the question in his heart. Then, he spoke.

"Guilt is like a shadow that lingers long after the sun has set. Even when the night has passed, even when we have learned, grown, and transformed—something within us holds onto the darkness. Why?"

The hall was silent, the weight of his words settling into every heart present.

The Unseen Shackles

"Once, there was a man who carried a stone upon his back. It was heavy, but he had grown so accustomed to it that he believed it was a part of him. One day, a wise traveller asked him, 'Why do you carry this burden?' The man replied, 'I was told long ago that I must. That I deserved to carry it.' The traveller smiled and said, 'But the one who gave it to you has long forgotten, and the road ahead is steep. Will you keep carrying it?' The man hesitated, then slowly placed the stone down. And for the first time in years, he walked freely.'"

Guruji paused, looking at each devotee in the hall.

"We hold onto guilt not because we must, but because we believe we must. We mistake it for responsibility, thinking that if we let go, we are dishonouring the lesson. But true wisdom is knowing when the lesson has been learned and when the burden is no longer needed."

The Prison of the Past

Guruji, with his voice deep with reverence.

Judas and Peter: The Crossroads of Guilt and Redemption

In **Matthew 27:3-5**, we see the tragic downfall of Judas Iscariot. After betraying Jesus for thirty pieces of silver, he is consumed by guilt. He returns the money to the chief priests, crying, *"I have sinned by betraying innocent blood."* But when they show him no mercy, he is overcome by despair and takes his own life.

"Then Judas, His betrayer, seeing that He had been condemned, was remorseful and brought back the thirty pieces of silver to the chief priests and elders, saying, 'I have sinned by betraying innocent blood.' And they said, 'What is that to us? You see to it!' Then he threw down the pieces of silver in the temple and departed, and went and hanged himself." — Matthew 27:35

Judas' guilt did not lead him to seek forgiveness. Instead, it became a noose—both metaphorically and literally—trapping him in despair. His remorse was deep, but it was not transformative.

Contrast this with Peter. In Luke 22:61-62, after denying Jesus three times, Peter meets the gaze of Christ and realises what he has done. Overcome with grief, he weeps bitterly.

"And the Lord turned and looked at Peter. Then Peter remembered the word of the Lord, how He had said to him, 'Before the rooster crows, you will deny Me three times.' So Peter went out and wept bitterly." — Luke 22:61-62

Yet, Peter's story does not end in despair. Unlike Judas, Peter's sorrow leads to redemption. In John 21:15-17, after the resurrection, Jesus asks Peter three times, *"Do you love Me?"*—symbolically undoing his three denials. Each time, Peter answers, *"Yes, Lord, You know that I love You,"* and Jesus commissions him: *"Feed My sheep."*

This is the key difference: Judas' guilt led him to self-destruction; Peter's guilt led him to transformation. One remained bound by regret, the other used it as a stepping stone to fulfil his purpose. Peter went on to become a pillar of faith, proving that guilt, when met with repentance and self-forgiveness, can be a force of renewal.

Arjuna and the Weight of Dharma: The Battle Against Guilt

In the Bhagavad Gita, Chapter 1 (Verses 28-30), Arjuna is paralysed by guilt before the battle of Kurukshetra. Seeing his own kin, teachers, and loved ones on the battlefield, he is overwhelmed with sorrow and despair.

"My whole body shudders, my mouth is dry, my limbs tremble, my skin burns. My bow slips from my hand, and my mind reels. I see only omens of misfortune, Krishna! I cannot bring myself to fight." — Bhagavad Gita 1:28-30

Arjuna fears that his actions, though righteous, will bring pain and destruction. He believes that by fighting, he will be sinning against his own bloodline. This moral conflict causes him to drop his weapons, surrendering not in wisdom but in despair.

Krishna, however, does not allow him to be consumed by guilt. In Bhagavad Gita 2:11, Krishna reminds Arjuna that true wisdom sees beyond temporary suffering:

"You grieve for those who should not be grieved for, yet you speak words of wisdom. The wise do not mourn for the living or the dead." — Bhagavad Gita 2:11

Then, in Bhagavad Gita 2:47, Krishna instructs Arjuna on the right mindset:

"Your right is to perform your duty only, but never to its fruits. Let not the fruits of action be your motive, nor let your attachment be to inaction." — Bhagavad Gita 2:47

Krishna urges Arjuna to act with a pure heart, free from guilt and attachment to outcomes. He teaches that guilt is an illusion when one's actions align with dharma (righteous duty). Unlike Judas, who was lost in despair, Arjuna learns to rise beyond his doubt and fulfil his role as a warrior.

The Lesson: Transforming Guilt Into Growth

Both Peter and Arjuna face moral crises. Both experienced guilt, but their response shaped their destiny. Peter chose faith over despair, and Arjuna chose dharma over hesitation. Their journeys remind us that guilt is not meant to chain us to the past but to guide us toward transformation.

True redemption does not come from endlessly punishing oneself but from using past mistakes as a foundation for wisdom and right action.

Guruji said, "Guilt is useful only when it awakens awareness, not when it imprisons the soul. When we have learned, when we have sought to make amends, when we have changed—then we must set it down. If not, it is no longer guilt—it is self-punishment."

The River Knows No Chains

"A river does not hold onto the debris it once carried. It flows onward, ever fresh, ever renewed. The past is not a prison—it is a teacher. When the lesson is learned, you do not stay in the classroom forever. You move forward."

He looked at Alice, his eyes filled with kindness.

"The question is not whether you have learned from your mistakes, but whether you are willing to let yourself be free of them."

The air in the hall felt lighter. A few devotees wiped their eyes. Somewhere outside, the wind stirred the trees, as if whispering—*"flow onward."*

The Journey to the Falls

As the afternoon sun softened under the shade of towering trees, the devotees meandered through the winding paths of the Kumbhariyur Estate. The air smelled of damp earth, the scent of jasmine and sandalwood lingering as a cool breeze wove through the dense foliage.

The meal had been simple yet fulfilling—warm rice, fragrant with ghee, dal thick with the richness of home, and freshly baked chapatis that melted in their mouths. But beyond the food, it was the silence that lingered, the kind that only deep introspection brings. Guruji's words from the morning session still echoed in their minds, settling in layers beneath their thoughts, stirring feelings they could not yet name.

Roopa's voice broke the quiet hum of rustling leaves. *"Today's session was very touching and deep."*

Abhirami nodded, her eyes carrying the weight of something unspoken. *"Yes, Roopa… It felt like Guruji was speaking directly to my heart."*

John stretched his arms and exhaled. *"Apeksha, we could have gone to the waterfall instead of sitting under the banyan tree."* His voice was light, yet carried the subtle desire to escape into nature.

Nita turned to him with a playful smirk. *"Well, we still have time until 6 P.M. We should go."*

The group exchanged glances, smiles growing on their lips.

"Then let's not waste a moment," Apeksha said, already stepping forward.

The path to the waterfall wound through ancient trees that had stood witness to time itself. Sunlight filtered through the canopy, painting shifting patterns on the ground. The distant sound of gurgling water grew louder with each step, an invitation pulling them forward.

As they walked, Dev ran his fingers along the rough bark of a tree, whispering, *"These trees have been here longer than any of us. Do you think they hold memories?"*

Aarna chuckled. *"Perhaps they do… if only we knew how to listen."*

Finally, they reached the clearing where the waterfall revealed itself—a silver ribbon cascading down jagged rocks, tumbling into an emerald pool below. Mist rose gently, catching the sunlight, creating halos of iridescent light. The water moved effortlessly, not resisting, not stopping—just flowing, forever embracing the path carved for it.

Vasudeva stood still, inhaling the crisp, damp air. His voice dropped to a whisper, almost as if speaking too loudly would disturb the sacred stillness. *"This place is tranquil…"*

Apeksha smiled, her gaze fixed on the water. *"And yet, it holds echoes of so many stories. Let me tell you one… an incident that happened right here, where Guruji helped someone find their way back from despair."*

Everyone settled onto the moss-covered rocks, eager to listen, as the waterfall continued its timeless symphony—whispering the secrets of surrender, of flow, of life itself.

"This place holds a story—a story of pain, surrender, and healing," she said, her voice carrying the weight of remembrance.

They all leaned in, listening intently.

"A few years ago, a man came here, lost in grief. His name was Raghav. He had lost his only son in an accident… a loss so unbearable that it hollowed him from within. He came to the ashram, but he could not sit through Guruji's teachings. He could not eat, could not sleep. Guilt clung to him like a shadow—guilt that he had sent his son out that day, guilt that he could not protect him."

She paused, watching the water flow endlessly over the rocks as if carrying away unseen burdens.

"One afternoon, Raghav walked alone to this very waterfall, intending to end his suffering. He stood at the edge, listening to the water, drowning in his sorrow. And that is when Guruji arrived."

John shifted uncomfortably. *"Did he… know?"* he asked.

Apeksha nodded. *"Guruji always knows."*

She continued, *"Guruji walked up to him, silent for a long time, just standing beside him. Then he spoke. 'Raghav, the water does not hold on to the rocks. It flows past them. Why do you hold on to pain that was meant to pass through you?'"*

Roopa whispered, *"And then?"*

Apeksha's eyes glistened. *"Raghav broke down. 'Guruji,' he cried, 'how can I let go? My son was my life. Without him, I am nothing.'"*

"Guruji placed a hand on his shoulder and said, 'You are not nothing, Raghav. You are a river that has forgotten its own flow. Your son was like a drop that returned to the ocean… but you remain stuck, clinging to the shore of grief. Let him go, not with sorrow, but with love.'"

Vasudeva exhaled as if the story itself had lifted something heavy off his heart.

"Raghav wept like the rain that day, and for the first time, he let the water cleanse his soul. He didn't jump. He didn't run away. He sat right here, letting the waterfall remind him that life moves forward, even after loss."

Aarna whispered, "And then?"

Apeksha smiled softly. "Raghav stayed at the ashram. Over time, he healed. He learned to live, not in the absence of grief, but in its acceptance. And you know what? He found purpose again—he now helps orphaned children, giving them the love he once poured into his son."

Silence hung between them, not heavy, but profound. The waterfall no longer seemed just a place of beauty—it carried echoes of someone's journey from darkness to light.

Kiran sighed, stretching his arms. *"Time for us to get back for the day's session."*

As they walked back, the waterfall behind them kept flowing, just as life did, just as it always would.

CHAPTER XI

The Enemy of Resistance

"Truth does not punish—it reflects. But we fear the mirror, for it shows us what we must release. Resistance is not against life—it is against seeing ourselves clearly."

– Shree Shambav

Synopsis

This chapter explores the subtle yet powerful force of avidya—ignorance—as the root of resistance. We resist change not because change itself is unbearable but because our illusions offer false comfort. Ignorance is not simply a lack of information; it is a refusal to see what must be seen. It keeps us clinging to the known, fearful of the truth that can transform us.

Through the questions of the devotees, Guruji guides the seekers to understand how resistance to truth delays healing and keeps the soul trapped in cycles of suffering. He shows that self-awareness, acceptance, and disciplined inner work are the keys to dissolving resistance. When we embrace truth—not just intellectually, but with surrender—we are set free. Liberation begins not when the world changes, but when we stop running from the light within.

Avidya - Ignorance, Avoiding Truth

Akshatha asked, "Guruji, why do we resist change, even when it is necessary?"

Guruji closed his eyes for a moment, as if reaching into a deeper space of remembrance, and then gently opened them with a soft smile.

"Akshatha, we resist change not because we don't long for freedom… but because we fear losing what we have known—even if what we know is pain."

Guruji said, "Imagine a bird born in a cage. Every morning, it wakes to the same bars, the same shadows, the same limited sky. One day, someone opens the cage door. But the bird does not fly out. Why? Because the unknown sky feels more dangerous than the familiar prison."

The Comfort of the Known

"We grow attached to the patterns we live in—even the ones that hurt us. We resist change because it demands the death of who we were. And dying, even symbolically, frightens the ego. Change threatens identity. If I am no longer this, then who am I? This is why we stay in unhealthy relationships, in jobs that numb our spirit, in beliefs that no longer serve the truth."

Lot's Wife – The Cost of Looking Back

"In *Genesis 19*, when God sent angels to rescue Lot and his family from the doomed city of Sodom, they were given one clear command: **'Flee and do not look back.'** The path ahead was uncertain, but salvation lay in moving forward.

Yet, as they escaped, Lot's wife turned back to gaze at the city she was leaving behind—and at that moment, she was turned into a pillar of salt.

Why? Her feet may have moved forward, but her heart was still trapped in the past. She longed for what was, even when what was had already been destroyed. Her resistance to change, her unwillingness to release what was familiar, became her undoing.

This is the lesson: **Clinging to the past can freeze us in place.** When we resist the flow of life, we become stuck—like salt, rigid and unmoving. To step into the future, we must stop feeding the illusion that the past is safer simply because it is familiar. Growth demands trust in what lies ahead, not longing for what has already crumbled."

The Nature of Water – Embracing Change

Lao Tzu, in the *Tao Te Ching*, said:

"Nothing in the world is as soft and yielding as water. Yet for dissolving the hard and inflexible, nothing can surpass it."

Guruji spoke gently, "Water does not fight the vessel that holds it—it adapts, flowing effortlessly into any shape. It does not resist change; it becomes one with it.

But what of the rock? The rock resists, unmoving, refusing to yield. And yet, over time, even the hardest stone is shaped, softened, and eventually worn away by the persistence of water.

Change is not your enemy—it is your nature. A river does not fight the course it must take; it flows. When you resist change, you are not protecting yourself—you are only delaying the inevitable. The moment you surrender to the flow of life, you realize that change was never a force against you, but a force shaping you into who you are meant to be."

The Illusion of Permanence – Breaking Free from Avidya

"In *Sankhya* philosophy and the *Upanishads*, ignorance (*avidya*) is the root of suffering. We mistake the temporary for the eternal, clinging to fleeting identities, possessions, and emotions. We say, 'I am this body, this name, this pain,' and in doing so, we bind ourselves to the illusion of permanence.

We resist change not because it harms us, but because it threatens the ego's fragile illusion of control. The ego whispers, 'Hold on—if you let go, you will lose yourself.' But the truth is, what is real can never be lost.

The Self is like the sun—unchanging, radiant, ever-present. When clouds gather, the sun does not disappear; it only seems hidden. Change is not destruction; it is the wind that clears the sky. If we trust it, if we allow it to move through us, we will see that nothing essential is ever taken away—only illusions are."

Guruji looked toward Akshatha, his voice now softer, soaked in compassion:

"To resist change is to deny the wisdom of your own becoming. You are not meant to stay where you are. Just as the seed must crack for the sprout to rise, so must we break open to become who we are meant to be. Pain may accompany change, but stagnation is suffering in silence. The soul whispers: evolve, evolve… And when we listen, we are carried—not by fear, but by grace."

The Veil of Ignorance – How Avidya Creates Suffering

Lalitha asked, "Guruji, how does ignorance perpetuate suffering and delusion?"

Lalitha's voice was soft, yet the weight of her question hung in the air. Guruji closed his eyes for a moment. "Ignorance is not the absence of knowledge—it is the refusal to see. It is like walking through a vast forest with our eyes tightly shut, stumbling over roots and thorns, cursing the pain, yet refusing to open our eyes and see the path before us."

The Rope and the Snake

Guruji smiled and said, "A man walking through the twilight. In the dim light, he sees a snake coiled in his path. Fear grips him—his heart races, sweat beads on his forehead. He turns to flee, but an old sage nearby calls out, 'Look again.' Trembling, the man hesitates, then takes a closer look. He realises—it is not a snake at all, but a coiled rope.

What changed? The object remained the same, but the man's *perception* shifted. His suffering did not come from reality but from his own misunderstanding of it. This is *avidya*, ignorance—the false narratives we create, the illusions we accept as truth, and the suffering they bring."

The Story of the Blindfold

Guruji continued, "A child, blindfolded as part of a game, stumbles and falls. She cries, fearing monsters and shadows. But the moment her blindfold is removed, the fear vanishes—because it was never real.

This is how *avidya* works. It blinds us, distorting our reality. We suffer not because the world is cruel, but because we refuse to see it clearly."

Guruji said, "In the Bible, when Jesus was crucified, he did not curse those who nailed him to the cross. Instead, he said, 'Father, forgive them, for they know not what they do.' (*Luke 23:34*) This is the tragedy of ignorance—it makes people act against truth, against love, against their nature. Those who live in darkness do not even realise they are blind. They suffer, and in their suffering, they cause suffering to others."

Guruji smiled and said, "When people believe they already have all the answers, they become difficult to teach. But when they recognize their own ignorance, they open themselves to true understanding."

He continued, "The wise do not grip tightly to false certainty. Like water, they remain open and adaptable, allowing truth to flow through them. But ignorance is like a clenched fist—rigid, unyielding, and full of struggle. The tighter we hold onto our illusions, the more we suffer."

The Awakening – Clearing the Mist

"Lalitha, ignorance is not a sin—it is a veil. A veil that covers the mind, making suffering inevitable. But like mist clearing in the morning sun, it can be lifted.

Knowledge, wisdom, and self-inquiry are the winds that disperse this fog.

If we question our fears, we may find they are ropes, not snakes. If we remove our blindfolds, we may see that the darkness was never real. And when we awaken, the suffering we once clung to will dissolve—like a dream fading at dawn."

Lalitha bowed her head, and her heart stirred. She now understood—ignorance is not an enemy to be fought but a darkness to be illuminated.

Breaking Through Resistance and Avoidance

Abhirami bowed and asked, "Guruji, what practices can break through resistance and avoidance?"

Guruji looked at her with kindness. "Resistance is like a locked door in the mind. We know that beyond it lies growth, healing, and transformation, yet we hesitate to step forward. Why? Because the familiar, even when painful, feels safer than the unknown."

Guruji said, "Imagine a cup is full of discoloured water—unchanged, unmoving. It cannot receive fresh water unless it is emptied. In the same way, we cannot move forward unless we release what holds us back. But how do we do this?"

Guruji said, "There was once a young sculptor named Lucas who lived in a small village. He had a rare gift—he could see statues hidden within raw stone before his chisel ever touched them. But one day, he received a large block of marble, and when he stood before it, doubt clouded his vision. He hesitated, unable to strike even a single blow.

'What if I ruin it?' he thought. 'What if this time, I fail?' Days passed, then weeks. The stone remained untouched, and his fear only deepened. It was not the marble that resisted transformation—it was Lucas."

Awareness: The First Step Toward Freedom

Guruji continued, "One evening, an old stonemason saw Lucas staring at the marble in frustration. He asked, 'Why have you not begun?'

Lucas replied, 'I cannot see the statue within. What if I make a mistake?'

The old man smiled. 'The statue is there, but your fear keeps you blind. You are not afraid of failure—you are afraid of what failure will mean about you.'

That night, Lucas reflected deeply. He realised it was not the stone that needed to change first—it was his own mind. His hesitation was not about skill but about self-doubt. This was his first moment of **awareness**: recognising that the resistance was within, not outside him.

Before we break through resistance, we must first **see it clearly**. Are we afraid of failure? Of pain? Of losing the image we hold of ourselves? **To name resistance is to loosen its grip.**"

Surrender: Becoming Like the Flowing River

"The next morning, Lucas picked up his chisel but hesitated again. The old stonemason watched and said, 'Why do you grip it so tightly? Let the chisel move as it must. Trust your hands.'

Lucas exhaled and softened his grip. He made his first strike—not with force, but with ease. His strokes became lighter, more fluid. For the first time, he allowed the stone to guide him.

Resistance thrives on control. We try to **force** certainty, to **fight** change, but like a river, transformation does not happen through force—it happens through flow.

When we surrender—not by giving up, but by trusting the process—we stop clinging to the illusion of control. Meditation, breathwork, and deep reflection help us soften our grip on fear. Like Lucas, we must loosen our hold and trust that **the form is already within the stone.**"

Action: The Fire That Transforms

"Days passed, and the marble began to take shape. The more Lucas worked, the more he realised: hesitation had been a greater burden than the work itself.

Finally, the statue stood complete—a masterpiece. He stepped back, eyes filled with wonder. The old stonemason smiled and said, 'The hardest part was never the carving. It was beginning.'

We do not overcome resistance by thinking our way out of it. We must **act**. A bird does not learn to fly by imagining the sky—it must leap.

If you fear speaking, say **one word**. If you avoid the truth, face **one reality**. If you fear failure, take **one step**.

Action dissolves hesitation. Movement clears the mist."

Guruji's voice softened. "The mind seeks comfort in the known, but the soul longs to grow. Resistance is not a wall—it is only a shadow that fades when we move toward it.

So tell me, Abhirami—what is the first small step you will take today?"

She looked up, eyes bright with realisation. The weight of hesitation had already begun to lift. The path was always there—she only needed to take the first step.

The Weight of Illusion

Roopa sat before Guruji, her eyes reflecting the silent battles of her soul. She took a deep breath and asked, "Guruji, how does embracing truth lead to liberation?"

Guruji looked at her with deep compassion and spoke gently.

"There was once a man named Suraj who carried a heavy sack wherever he went. Day and night, he bore its weight—on his shoulders, in his heart. People often asked, 'What do you carry?' But he only clutched it tighter, saying, 'These are the pieces of my past, my regrets, my unspoken truths. If I let them go, who will I be?'

One day, he met an old sage who watched him struggle under the burden. The sage asked, 'Open the sack. See what you are carrying.'

Reluctantly, Suraj untied the knot. And inside, he found—nothing.

The weight he had suffered under for years was never real. It was only the illusion of his unspoken truths, the lies he had told himself, the fears he had refused to face.

Tears welled in his eyes. The moment he **saw the truth**, he was free."

The Illusion That Binds Us

Guruji continued, "In the **Bible - John 8:32**, Jesus said, *'You will know the truth, and the truth will set you free.'* But why does truth bring freedom? Because **what binds us is not reality but illusion.**

A prisoner bound by real chains struggles against iron. But most of us are trapped not by metal, but by the stories we tell ourselves:

- *'I am not enough.'*
- *'I cannot change.'*
- *'If I face the truth, I will break.'*

These thoughts are like shadows in a dark room—frightening until we turn on the light. When we resist truth, we live in fear of what we might see. But when we embrace it, we realise it was never the truth itself that hurt us—it was the running, the hiding, the denial."

The Mirror of Reality

Guruji asked, "If you look into a disturbed lake, what do you see?"

Roopa shook her head. "Nothing clear. Only ripples and distortions."

Guruji nodded. "This is the mind clouded by avoidance. When we run from truth, our minds remain in turmoil. We cannot see ourselves clearly.

But if you let the water settle—what then?"

She smiled. "I would see my true reflection."

Guruji said, "When the mind is still, the Self reveals itself like the moon reflected in a quiet lake."

Truth is like still water—it reflects who we truly are. When we stop running, when we sit with ourselves, clarity emerges. And in that clarity, there is peace."

Walking Through the Fire

"But embracing truth is not always gentle," Guruji continued. "Sometimes, it is fire.

Guruji said, "A young blacksmith who feared the forge. He wished to shape metal but dreaded the flames. One day, his master said, 'If you wish to craft something strong, you must let the fire temper it.

Likewise, truth may burn at first—it may expose wounds, shake illusions, and demand change. But if we walk through that fire, we emerge stronger, like steel refined."

He paused, his voice deepening. *"Truth does not break us. It breaks what was false within us."*

Roopa closed her eyes, feeling the weight of her own unspoken truths.

Guruji said, "The moment Suraj opened his sack and saw the emptiness within, he was free. The moment you face what you fear, you will see: there is no prison—only the walls we build ourselves.

Liberation is not given to us—it is revealed when we stop hiding from what already is."

PART FOUR

THE VICTORY

DISCOVERING THE TRUTH

"The greatest battles are not fought with swords or words, but within the silent chambers of the soul. To conquer the world is fleeting, but to conquer oneself is eternal victory."

-Shree Shambav

CHAPTER XII

The Path to Liberation

"You do not find truth—you remember it. Like the sun behind the clouds, it was never gone, only waiting for the winds of awareness to clear the sky."

– Shree Shambav

Synopsis

The journey has led to its final test, where the greatest battle is fought—not against the world, but within. The struggles with doubt, fear, and illusion have shaped the path, revealing deeper truths along the way. Now, the moment of realisation arrives.

What does it mean to truly conquer the inner enemies? How can victory be sustained in the endless battle of the mind? What lies beyond fear, doubt, and illusion? And how can one's journey become a guiding light for others still searching?

Liberation is not about reaching a distant destination but awakening to a truth that was always present. The war was never external—it was always within. The greatest victory is not in overcoming something outside but in remembering who we truly are. The path does not end here; it only expands into infinity.

The Battle Within: Conquering the Inner Enemies

As the evening sun cast long golden shadows over the ashram, the devotees sat in silent anticipation. The air was thick with the scent of incense, the faint sound of a temple bell ringing in the distance. Akshaya's voice broke the silence.

"Guruji, what does it mean to conquer the inner enemies?"

Guruji sat still for a moment, gazing at the flickering lamp before him. Then, he spoke, *"My child, the greatest battles are not fought on the fields of war but within the chambers of the mind. To conquer the inner enemies is not to destroy them with force, but to transform them with wisdom."*

He paused, letting the weight of his words settle. Then, Guruji began a story.

The Warrior and the Shadow

"There was once a great warrior who had fought and won many battles. Kings feared him, and enemies trembled at the mention of his name. Yet, despite his victories, he was restless. Something gnawed at him, an unease he could not name.

One night, as he sat by the river, an old sage appeared before him. 'You have conquered the world, but have you conquered yourself?' the sage asked.

The warrior scoffed. 'What do you mean? I fear no enemy!'

The sage smiled. 'Then sit with me until dawn, and I will show you your greatest enemy.'

As the night deepened, shadows flickered around them. Suddenly, the warrior saw something moving—a dark figure mirroring his every movement.

'What is that?' he demanded.

The sage replied, 'That is your Shadow—the fear, anger, greed, pride, and doubt that have always lived within you. It has fought every battle beside you, unseen but never absent.'

The warrior gripped his sword. 'Then I will slay it.'

The sage laughed. 'Foolish one. Can you strike down your own reflection in the water? Your shadow is not to be killed but understood. Do not fight it. Sit with it. Listen.'

So the warrior sat. He watched the shadow dance, flicker, and shift. And slowly, he recognised its shapes—the moments of rage, the wounds of rejection, the fear of being unworthy.

And then, something strange happened. As he accepted his shadow, it softened. It no longer controlled him, no longer dictated his battles. By morning, the warrior understood: the greatest conquest is not of lands or people, but of the self."

The Five Enemies

Guruji let the story linger before he spoke again.

"we all have inner enemies—fear, pride, greed, attachment, and ignorance. They do not live outside of us; they reside within.

1. **Fear** binds us, making us small when we were meant to be vast.

2. **Pride** blinds us, making us believe we are separate from truth.

3. **Greed** traps us in endless hunger, never letting us rest.

4. **Attachment** makes us cling to things that are fleeting, causing suffering.

5. **Ignorance** keeps us from seeing that we are more than our thoughts and desires.

To conquer them does not mean to fight them with violence. It means to see them, to understand them, and to transform them. When you hold a lamp in a dark room, the darkness does not resist—it simply disappears."

Guruji smiled. *"The true battle is never outside of us. It is here"—he tapped his heart—" and here"—he pointed to his mind. "Conquer the self, and you have already won the greatest war."*

The devotees sat in silence, the truth settling deep within them. Akshaya felt a shift, as if a door had opened inside his soul. For the first time, he understood—the enemy was never outside. It had always been within.

Sustaining Victory in the Battle Within

Padma, her voice steady but filled with curiosity, asked,

"Guruji, how can we sustain victory in the battle within?"

Guruji closed his eyes for a moment as if listening to something beyond the silence.

The Warrior Who Forgot His Strength

Guruji said, "Once, there was a warrior who fought a great battle within himself—against fear, against doubt, against his own restless mind. With great effort, he conquered his inner enemies and stood victorious.

At first, he walked with confidence, his spirit light, his heart free. But as time passed, his old habits whispered to him. Shadows of doubt crept back into his mind.

The warrior, once fearless, began to question himself again.

One day, he approached his old master and said, 'I have won the battle, but I feel as though I am losing once more. How can I keep my victory?'

The master smiled and took him to a well. He pointed to the reflection in the water. 'Look at yourself. What do you see?'

The warrior replied, 'I see myself, but the water is disturbed by ripples.'

The master dropped a heavy stone into the well. The ripples grew larger, distorting the image.

'This is your mind when you forget your practice,' the master said. 'Victory is not a destination; it is a path you must walk every day. Just as the water clears when left undisturbed, so too must you return to stillness again and again.'"

The Three Pillars of Sustaining Victory

Guruji opened his eyes and continued, his voice steady as the wind that moves the river but does not disturb its depth.

"Sustaining victory over the mind is not a single battle—it is a lifelong journey. There are three

pillars that hold this victory steady: Awareness, Discipline, and Devotion."

Awareness: The Light That Never Sleeps

Guruji looked at Padma and the others, his eyes glimmering with wisdom.

Let me tell you a story of a man who lived in darkness without realizing it.

There was once a sculptor who worked in a dimly lit workshop. Every day, he chiselled away at stones, believing he was creating masterpieces. But because he had never seen his work in the full light of day, he never noticed the cracks and imperfections in his sculptures.

One day, a friend invited him outside. The sculptor hesitated—he feared that the sunlight would expose his flaws. But when he finally stepped into the light, he saw his statues clearly. Some were beautiful, others were broken. He realised that all his life, he had been shaping blindly.

Likewise, the mind works in darkness when it lacks awareness. Doubt, fear, and attachments thrive in the shadows, feeding on what we do not see. But when you bring light to your thoughts—when you observe them without judgment—you take away their power over you.

Awareness is not about fighting your thoughts; it is about seeing them clearly. The light of awareness reveals the truth, and once the truth is seen, it cannot be unseen."

Padma nodded, understanding now that victory begins with the courage to see things as they are.

Discipline: The Sword That Must Stay Sharp

Guruji said, "Many warriors have won great battles but lost their way because they failed to maintain discipline.

Once, a monk climbed to the top of a mountain to meditate. He sat in stillness for years, untouched by worldly distractions. One day, he thought, 'I have conquered my mind. I am free.'

So, he descended from the mountain and entered a village. At first, he remained peaceful. But soon, small irritations crept in—someone pushed past him in the market, a merchant overcharged him, a child mocked his robe. Frustration and anger slowly returned. Within days, the peace he had cultivated for years was lost.

Why? Because victory is not a place you reach—it is a practice you sustain. Just as a sword will rust if not sharpened, the mind will return to chaos if not disciplined.

Discipline is not punishment—it is protection. A daily practice of meditation, self-reflection, and restraint keeps the inner enemies at bay. The battle within is never won by force, but by daily, mindful effort."

The devotees sat in silence, realising that the greatest challenge was not winning once but choosing victory every day.

Devotion: The Fire That Never Fades

Guruji's voice softened.

"Even the strongest warrior grows weary. But if his heart is devoted to truth, his spirit will never tire.

There was once a great musician who played the flute so beautifully that even the trees swayed to his melody. But one day, he lost his flute. In despair, he sat in silence, believing he had lost his gift.

An old sage approached and asked, 'Why do you weep?'

'I have lost my flute,' the musician said. 'Without it, I cannot create music.'

The sage smiled and touched his heart. 'The music was never in the flute—it was always within you.'

Devotion is not about clinging to a practice, a place, or a ritual. It is about surrendering to something greater than yourself. When you dedicate your life to truth, whether you call it Divine, the Tao, the Shambav (Mahaspanda) or the Self, you are carried by a force beyond exhaustion.

If you walk with devotion, you will never truly fall."

Note: Shambav – The sacred emergence of the auspicious, the divine unfolding of truth, and the transcendental awakening of the soul.

Guruji leaned forward, his voice a whisper that carried the weight of the universe.

"Victory is not a single moment of triumph. It is the breath you take each morning, the choice you make in every moment. It is the courage to return to the path, even when you stumble.

The warrior who sustains his victory is not the one who never falls, but the one who never stops rising."

Padma felt something shift deep within her. She understood now—the way to sustain victory was to live it, moment by moment, with awareness, discipline, and devotion.

The Truth Beyond Fear, Doubt, and Illusions

Nita asked, "Guruji, what is the truth beyond fear, doubt, and illusions?"

Nita's voice was steady, yet there was a quiet tremor beneath her words.

Guruji closed his eyes for a moment, then opened them with a gaze so still, so deep, that it felt like looking into eternity.

The Parable of the Shadow

Guruji began, "Imagine a child walking alone at dusk. The sun sinks lower, and behind her, her own shadow stretches—long, dark, menacing. She is afraid. The more she runs, the larger the shadow grows, chasing her like a silent predator.

But then—what happens when she turns around?

She faces the sun. And in that moment, the shadow disappears behind her."

Guruji paused, letting the image settle in their minds.

"Our fears, our doubts, our illusions—they are shadows. They only exist when we turn away from the light of truth. The more we run from them, the stronger they seem. But the moment we turn inward and face reality with courage, they lose their power."

The Nature of Fear and Illusion

Guruji continued, "Fear is born from attachment. We fear loss because we believe something belongs to us. We fear uncertainty because we cling to control. We fear judgment because we mistake our identity for the image we project to the world.

But tell me—can the sky fear the storm? The storm may pass through it, but the sky remains untouched. The true Self is like that sky—vast, infinite, unaffected. The illusions of the mind may create tempests, but they do not alter the truth of who we are."

The devotees sat in quiet reflection. Some lowered their heads. Others gazed at the floor as if contemplating the weight of their own fears.

The Man in the Mirror

Guruji, after a pause, said, "Once, there was a man who woke up every morning and looked in the mirror. But instead of seeing his own face, he saw a monster. He tried to wash it away, but the reflection remained. He avoided mirrors, covered them with cloth, refused to see his image.

One day, he went to a wise sage and said, 'I am cursed. Every time I look into a mirror, I see a beast staring back at me.'

The sage smiled and handed him a bowl of water. 'Look inside,' he said.

The man looked—and in the gentle ripples, he saw his true face.

The sage explained, 'Your mind is the mirror. When it is clouded with fear, self-doubt, and illusion, you cannot see yourself clearly. But when the waters are still, your true nature is reflected perfectly.'"

The Truth Beyond the Mind

Guruji's voice softened. "The truth beyond fear, doubt, and illusion is simple—you are not what your mind tells you.

You are not your failures.
You are not your fears.
You are not the doubts that whisper in your heart.
You are something far greater.
Beneath the layers of fear, beyond the illusions woven by the mind, there is a stillness—a deep, unshakable knowing. That is the truth. That is who you are."

Nita felt something shift within her, like a veil being lifted. She had spent years battling her fears, trying to silence the doubts that haunted her. But now, she understood—she didn't have to fight them. She only had to turn and face the sun.

The hall was silent, yet it was the kind of silence that felt full, alive. It was as if something invisible, something profound, had just been spoken—not in words, but in the very air they breathed.

Guruji smiled gently. "Truth does not need to be found—it only needs to be seen."

The Ripple of a Single Step

Apeksha's voice was gentle yet filled with a quiet urgency. "Guruji, how can our journey inspire others to embark on their own path?"

Guruji closed his eyes briefly, as if feeling the weight of the question in his heart. Then, with a deep breath, he opened them and began, his voice steady, rich with wisdom.

The Lamp That Lights Another

"A lamp does not teach darkness how to become light. It simply shines. And in its presence, the darkness fades."

He paused, letting the words settle. "A true seeker does not inspire others by preaching or persuading. Instead, they become living examples of truth, and that truth calls to those who are ready. Just as one candle lights another without losing its own flame, your journey will touch the hearts of others—not by force, but by its very radiance."

Apeksha listened, her heart steady, yet something within her stirred—a longing to understand more deeply.

The Story of the Silent Monk

Guruji continued, "There was once a monk who lived in solitude, high in the mountains. He never spoke of wisdom, never wrote scriptures, never taught a single lesson. Yet, people travelled from distant lands just to be in his presence.

One day, a young man, confused by this, asked him, 'Master, why do so many seek you when you have never spoken a word of teaching?'

The monk simply smiled and led the young man to a frozen river. There, he took a stone and placed it on the ice. The young man watched as the stone remained motionless, unaffected.

Then, the monk took another stone and placed it in the flowing water of a nearby stream. Slowly, gently, the current carried it forward.

Looking into the young man's eyes, the monk finally spoke. 'Wisdom is not taught; it is lived. Be like the flowing river, and others will follow its course.'"

Your Steps Become a Path

Guruji turned his gaze toward Apeksha. "Do not worry about how to inspire others. Instead, walk your path with sincerity, with depth, with truth. When people see transformation—not in your words, but in your presence, in your actions, in your very being—they will feel something stir within themselves.

And that feeling will not come from you; it will come from the truth within them. You are merely a reminder, a reflection of what they have always carried inside."

Apeksha felt something shift inside her. How often had she tried to explain, to convince, to lead others onto the path of self-discovery? But now, she understood. She did not have to lead—she simply had to walk.

The Story of the Wounded Bird

Guruji smiled softly and said, "Once, there was a bird with a broken wing. It longed to fly, but every time it tried, it collapsed in pain. It began to believe it would never soar again.

One day, as it sat in despair, it noticed another bird—one that had once been wounded, just as it was. This bird had scars, yet it flew with strength, with grace.

The wounded bird thought to itself, 'If that one could heal, perhaps I can too.'

And so, for the first time, it tried again.

And this time, it did not fall."

Guruji's voice was almost a whisper now. "You do not need to tell others to rise. You only need to rise yourself. And in seeing you, they will remember that they, too, have wings."

The Final Realisation

Apeksha felt a deep stillness within her. She understood now—the greatest way to inspire was not through grand speeches or endless explanations. It was through being.

Through living with truth.
Through walking with love.
Through healing, and showing that healing is possible.

Guruji smiled as if he already knew she had found her answer. "Your journey is not just yours. Every step you take clears the way for someone else. Walk with faith, and the path will unfold for many."

WRAP UP

The Inner Battlefield

The Silent Departure

The hush that fell upon the hall was not mere silence—it was a presence, an unspoken understanding that stretched between every soul gathered. Guruji sat with his eyes closed, his breath steady, his very stillness a teaching in itself.

The devotees watched him, their own breaths unconsciously mirroring the rhythm of his. Time no longer felt linear; it softened, stretched, dissolved. In that moment, there were no questions, no doubts, no seeking. Just being.

Guruji opened his eyes. A soft smile played upon his lips—not one of parting, but of knowing. As though he had already placed within them everything they needed.

With effortless grace, he rose. The rustling of his robes was the only sound, a whisper of movement that carried the weight of eternity. He did not speak. There was nothing left to say. And yet, in that silence, he spoke everything.

He turned, walking toward the exit, his presence neither diminishing nor departing—it only spread, like the fragrance of incense after the flame has been extinguished. His steps were unhurried, as if each footfall was a final blessing upon the ground he walked.

A Reflection on the Journey

No one moved. It was as if Guruji's stillness had become their own, their bodies and minds reluctant to disturb the sacred space that had just been created. The moment stretched, not in sorrow, but in reverence. It was not an ending but a quiet awakening.

One by one, they stirred, their gestures slow, their eyes brimming with something unnamed yet deeply felt. Some looked toward the doorway where Guruji had vanished, half-expecting to see him standing there still. Others lowered their gaze inward, recognising that his presence had not left them—it had merely shifted from the external to the eternal.

The Shambav Hall, once filled with voices, now held only echoes—of wisdom, of laughter, of tears shed in understanding. Yet it felt fuller than ever, its walls bearing witness to transformation. The space itself had changed, or perhaps it was they who had changed.

The Fire Within: A Retreat's End, A Journey's Beginning

The silence was thick, not with emptiness, but with reflection. The embers of the day's wisdom still burned within each heart. It was Rohith who finally spoke, his voice steady yet carrying the weight of reverence.

"This retreat has been more than a lesson—it's been a mirror." He paused, letting the words settle like ripples upon still water. "The core enemies Guruji spoke of on the first day—Desire, Anger, Greed, Attachment, Pride, and Jealousy—were not just abstract concepts. His stories, simple yet profound, struck straight into the depths of our hearts."

Heads nodded in agreement. Each of them had felt it—those quiet revelations, those sharp pangs of truth cutting through their illusions.

Lalitha spoke next, his tone contemplative. "And the second day… The session on the final battle—Fear, Doubt, Guilt, and Resistance. It was a revelation. I had spent years battling shadows, thinking my enemies were outside me. But Guruji showed me they were within… and far greater than I ever imagined."

A moment of silence. Then, a ripple of soft laughter—light, knowing, like the breaking of chains.

Padma stretched, looking around at the glowing faces, the unspoken gratitude in their eyes. "Let's have dinner. Then let's gather by the fireplace."

Under the Starlit Sky

Later that evening, they sat encircling a crackling fire. The night stretched endlessly above them, stars scattered like whispers of forgotten dreams. The flames flickered, casting shadows that danced upon their faces, illuminating eyes still lost in thought.

Sam, gazing at the fire, exhaled deeply. "Let me share an incident from a past retreat… an evening much like this one."

The group leaned in, the anticipation unspoken yet palpable.

"I still remember it vividly. A man had come to the retreat—Rohan. He was respected, successful, but something about him felt… caged. He carried himself with pride, but his eyes betrayed him. They were restless, searching. One evening, after a session, he approached Guruji and asked, 'Guruji, why do I feel like I have everything, yet nothing at all?'

Guruji had smiled gently, looking at him as though he had already seen the answer buried deep within. He did not answer immediately. Instead, he pointed to the small oil lamp beside him.

'*Blow it out,*' he said.

Confused but obedient, Rohan blew gently. The flame flickered, hesitated, then extinguished, leaving behind a thin, winding trail of smoke.

Guruji then picked up the lamp and turned it upside down. A thick stream of unburned oil poured onto the earth.

'*Tell me, Rohan,*' Guruji said softly. '*Was the flame the source of light, or was it the oil?*'

Rohan frowned. 'The oil feeds the flame. Without oil, there is no fire.'

Guruji nodded. '*And what if the oil had remained untouched? Would it have ever fulfilled its purpose?*'

Realisation dawned upon Rohan's face, but Guruji continued.

'*Many live like this unburned oil—possessing everything yet remaining unlit. They accumulate wealth, achievements, and status, yet something feels missing. Because they have never set themselves on fire for something greater than themselves. Rohan, you are full—but you are not burning.*'

Sam's voice softened. "That night, Rohan wept. Not out of sorrow, but out of understanding. The next morning, he sat in meditation longer than anyone else. When he left the retreat, he was not the same man. I heard later that he gave up chasing meaningless pursuits and began working with underprivileged children. He had found his fire."

A deep silence followed, stretching beyond words. The flames crackled, and the stars seemed to listen.

A Journey That Never Ends

After a long discussion, they sat in quiet reflection. Guruji's teachings, the stories shared, the laughter and the tears—all had woven themselves into something permanent, something unseen but deeply felt.

This retreat was not an end. It was a beginning. A seed planted deep within the soil of their souls, waiting to bloom.

One by one, they stood, stretching, murmuring quiet goodnights. As they dispersed, walking back through the moonlit paths, they carried with them something precious. Not just wisdom, but a quiet, persistent reminder—to live simply, to live intentionally, to live meaningfully.

They would stumble—of course, they would. That was the nature of the path. But now they carried within them the tools to rise again.

The retreat had ended. But the journey?

The journey had only just begun.

Life Coach and Philanthropist

Shree Shambav is the visionary founder of the Shree Shambav Ayur Rakshita Foundation (www.shambav-ayurrakshita.org). He founded this institution with a lofty goal: to recognise human identity across gender, ethnicity, and nationality. Through this organisation, he wants to assist all communities in realising their full potential and the intrinsic beauty of life.

Shree Shambav, a Life Coach, is dedicated to supporting people on their journeys of self-discovery and empowerment. He assists people in discovering who they are, determining what inspires and drives them, and overcoming limiting ideas. His approach clarifies what one wants in life, assisting people through goal-setting and a step-by-step process for achieving them. He empowers people to make deliberate and responsible decisions, allowing them to identify their blind spots and evolve as individuals via the use of numerous strategies and tools.

The foundation's bold, uncompromising, and compassionate ventures are always aimed at initiating the “Inner Transformation” process. They focus on spiritual growth, personal growth, and self-healing while emphasising that true progress lies in “Inclusive Growth and Co-existence.” This philosophy drives all their initiatives, encouraging a holistic approach to development and well-being.

Under Shree Shambav’s leadership, the foundation has launched several impactful movements:

Shree Shambav Green Movement: This mission is to create a healthy, green, and clean earth through responsible water conservation and greening initiatives. The movement strives to make the world a green paradise by encouraging sustainable living and environmental responsibility.

Shree Shambav Vidya Vedhika (Vizhuthugal): This project aims to help students and children by offering training, books, stationery, and uniforms. It aims to provide the next generation with the tools and resources they need to excel both academically and personally.

Shree Shambav and his foundation exemplify the spirit of compassion, transformation, and inclusive growth via their work, which has a profound impact on individuals and communities around the world. His work exemplifies the power of acknowledging and nourishing the human spirit, creating a world in which everyone can reach their full potential and appreciate the beauty of life.

TESTIMONIALS

Journey of Soul - Karma - "We die in our twenties and are buried at eighty." Remember that nothing can stop someone who refuses to be stopped. "Most people do not fail; they simply give up." Shree Shambav deserves full credit. It allowed me to sit and consider what I might miss out on in life. The author has delved into every aspect of our daily lives. How can a seemingly insignificant change in these seemingly insignificant details bring us such joy? The Soul of Journey teaches you the "art of living" as well as the "art of dying."

Twenty + One Series - The rich cultural heritage offered a host in twenty + one short stories with incredible imagination, morals and values prevalent at a given time, influencing how people respond to a crisis or any situation. The author has recreated images with universal values and morals. The plentiful of fascinating from faraway lands would leave the modern play and story writers a cringe. The book supports trust and immeasurable values instilling hope for the new generations.

Death - "Shree Shambav's 'Death - Light of Life and the Shadow of Death' is an extraordinary masterpiece that delves deep into the profound questions surrounding our existence and mortality. The book's opening statement, 'Nothing ever truly dies; it simply ceases to exist in one form before resuming it in another,' sets the stage for a thought-provoking exploration of death's multifaceted nature. Shambav's remarkable ability to navigate the philosophical complexities of death and our universal fear of it is both enlightening and comforting. This book is a testament to the power of understanding and acceptance."

Whispers of Eternity - "Reading 'Whispers of Eternity' by Shree Shambav was a transformative experience that left me captivated from beginning to end. Each section of this exquisite collection delves into the myriad facets of existence, offering poignant reflections on life, death, and everything in between. Shree Shambav's verses are a testament to the beauty of language and the power of expression, inviting readers to embark on a journey of self-discovery and spiritual awakening. Whether celebrating life's simple joys or grappling with the complexities of human emotion, this book is a timeless companion that speaks to the heart and soul of every reader."

Life Changing Journey Series - "Life Changing Journey Series II Inspirational Quotes" is a remarkable collection that illuminates the path to self-discovery and personal growth. With its inspiring quotes and insightful reflections, this book serves as a beacon of light in a world often shrouded in darkness. Each quote offers wisdom, guidance, and encouragement, reminding readers of their inner strength and resilience. A must-read for anyone seeking inspiration and enlightenment.

Learn To Love Yourself – "A Heartfelt Guide to Authentic Self-Love." "Learn to Love Yourself" invites readers on a transformative journey to embrace their true essence in a world often focused on external validation. Through ten insightful chapters, it gently reveals principles of genuine self-love, guiding readers to deepen their connection with themselves. Beyond surface positivity, it encourages the cultivation of resilient self-acceptance, from embracing one's unique qualities to setting empowering boundaries. With inspiring stories and practical wisdom, this book is a trusted companion on the path to inner peace, fulfilment, and joy, helping readers build lives that reflect their authentic selves.

The Power of Letting Go – This book has been a gift to my spiritual journey. Shree Shambav's insights into attachment, personal growth cycles, and forgiveness are enlightening. The concept of seven-year cycles resonated with me, helping me understand the natural phases of life. I feel more empowered to let go of what no longer serves me and step into a life of freedom and fulfilment. A truly beautiful read!

A Journey of Lasting Peace – "A Journey of Lasting Peace" feels like a trusted friend guiding you through the maze of self-discovery. The 18 transformative principles are both practical and deeply resonant, addressing everything from gratitude practices to the art of letting go. Each chapter is infused with warmth and wisdom, making it easy to apply the concepts to my life. I particularly appreciated the emphasis on physical health's connection to mental well-being; it served as a wake-up call for me to prioritize my health. This book is an invaluable resource for anyone serious about personal growth!

Astrology Unveiled Series – "Profound, Logical, and Inspiring". What stands out in Astrology Unveiled is the author's dedication to making Vedic astrology logical and approachable. Each concept flows naturally into the next, backed by examples and exercises. The insights into karma and life cycles add a philosophical depth rarely seen in astrology books. Perfect for anyone seeking spiritual growth alongside astrological knowledge!

The Entitlement Trap - "Thought-Provoking and Challenging" The book challenges readers to confront their own sense of entitlement, and that's not easy—but it's essential. The Entitlement Trap doesn't offer a one-size-fits-all approach. Instead, it's a thoughtful, layered examination of how entitlement can limit our growth. The chapter on "Defining Your Own Hill" was particularly impactful, as it pushed me to reconsider which challenges are truly worth pursuing. A thought-provoking read for those willing to do the inner work to create a life they can be proud of.

Whispers of a Dying Soul – "A Soul-Stirring Reflection on Life's Unspoken Truths" **-** *Whispers of a Dying Soul: Unspoken Regrets and Unlived Dreams"* is a deeply moving exploration of the unexpressed emotions and unfulfilled aspirations that shape our lives in ways we often don't realise. This book invites readers to confront the powerful, often hidden impact of regret while guiding them through a journey of introspection and healing. Each page opens a space to reflect on the choices that define us—from moments of unspoken love to neglected passions—offering a gentle reminder to live authentically and courageously.

Whispers of the Soul: A Journey Through Haiku - is a mesmerising collection that speaks directly to the heart. Each haiku is a delicate brushstroke capturing life's fleeting beauty and timeless wisdom, inviting readers into moments of deep reflection and peace. This book is a balm for the soul, guiding us to find meaning in stillness and connection in simplicity. The themes of nature, love, and mindfulness echo universal truths, resonating with quiet, powerful grace. It's a book to be savoured slowly, cherished deeply, and returned to often. Truly, a gift for anyone seeking calm and clarity in life's chaos.

Whispers of Silence - Unlocking Inner Power through Stillness by Shree Shambav is a rare gem that beckons readers to pause, reflect, and reconnect with their inner selves. In a world that never stops talking, this book offers a profound exploration of silence—not as a void but as a rich and transformative space.

From the first page, Shree Shambav's writing resonates deeply, blending scientific insights with spiritual wisdom in a way that feels both universal and deeply personal. The author's ability to bridge the tangible and the transcendent makes this book an invaluable guide for anyone navigating the chaos of modern life.

The Power of Words: Transforming Speech, Transforming Lives - "The Power of Words is a profound and enlightening guide that has transformed the way I approach communication. Shree Shambav masterfully uncovers the hidden influence of our words on relationships, self-perception, and overall well-being. This book doesn't just teach you how to speak; it inspires mindful communication that fosters connection and trust. The insights on replacing negative patterns like gossip and judgment with kindness and authenticity are truly life-changing. The practical strategies and engaging narratives make it an invaluable resource for personal and professional growth. A must-read for anyone striving to communicate with intention, clarity, and compassion. Highly recommended!"

The Art of Intentional Living: Minimalism for a Life of Purpose - "The Art of Intentional Living is a refreshing guide to finding clarity in a cluttered world. With practical wisdom and profound insights, it inspires you to simplify, prioritise, and live with purpose. A must-read for anyone seeking balance and fulfilment."

Awakening the Infinite: The Power of Consciousness in Transforming Life - "Awakening the Infinite is a transformative guide that expands the mind and nourishes the soul. With profound insights and practical wisdom, this book beautifully explores the power of consciousness, helping readers connect with their true purpose and inner potential. It is a journey of self-discovery, healing, and spiritual awakening, offering clarity and inspiration at every turn. A must-read for anyone looking to live with greater awareness, meaning, and authenticity."

ACKNOWLEDGEMENTS

To my grandfathers, grandmothers, mothers, fathers, aunts, uncles, neighbours, sisters, brothers, friends, and teachers, they poured in endless moral stories, retellings of Ramayana, Mahabharata, Puranas, Upanishads, and so on.

My teachers, neighbours, and kindred souls. Who provided us with a stage to perform wonderful Puranic stories and were gracious enough to acknowledge our efforts.

The artists and translators of epics have served as a source of inspiration, invigorating our spirits, making these works accessible, and enabling us to grasp the profound depths and deeper dimensions they contain.

I also cherish the stimulating conversations; I had with my wonderful mothers, Punitha Muniswamy and Uma Devi.

Our family's youngest member, Aadhya, who always overwhelmed me with questions, inspired this book.

I would likewise prefer to express gratitude to Mr Sivakumar, Mrs Roopa Sivakumar, Mr Akshaya Rajesh, Ms Akshatha Rajesh, Ms Apeksha Prabhu, Mr

Akanksh Prabhu, Mr Nikash Sarasambi, Mrs Spoorthi Nikash for their valuable inputs.

I must thank Mr Rajesh, Mr Savan Prabhu, Mrs Revathi Rajesh, Mrs Rajani Sarasambi, and Mrs Manju Reshma, who encouraged me and often suggested writing a book. Their unwavering belief that I had something valuable to offer kept me going during my writing sessions.

Love you all,

Shree Shambav

www.shambav.org

shreeshambav@gmail.com

BOOKS BY - AUTHOR

Journey of Soul - KARMA

"Journey of Soul – Karma" is a heartfelt exploration of life's profound truths in our increasingly complex world. Addressing challenges, inequalities, and the quest for meaning, this book brings the timeless concept of Karma into focus. It emphasizes Karma not merely as philosophy, but as a guiding principle for our daily lives, inspiring us to walk a path of integrity and purpose. Through this journey, readers gain insights into how actions shape destinies, encouraging a life aligned with truth and compassion. It's a beacon for those seeking a deeper, more fulfilled existence.

Death - Light of Life and the Shadow of Death

In *Light of Life and the Shadow of Death*, the enigma of mortality is approached with clarity and compassion. Death is an inevitable certainty, yet it casts a lingering shadow of fear over our lives, stirring grief and despair as we strive to prolong our time on earth. This profound work examines the fate of departed souls and the heavy emotions we attach to loss. Yet, it offers a path toward accepting death and finding peace amid life's uncertainties. Exploring our origins, ethical values, and purpose, it unveils the sustaining truth of existence. The shadow of death, though daunting, is reframed as a shared, universal experience—one that calls us to confront our deepest fears with wisdom and grace.

Whispers of Eternity 150 Plus - A Symphony of Soulful Verses

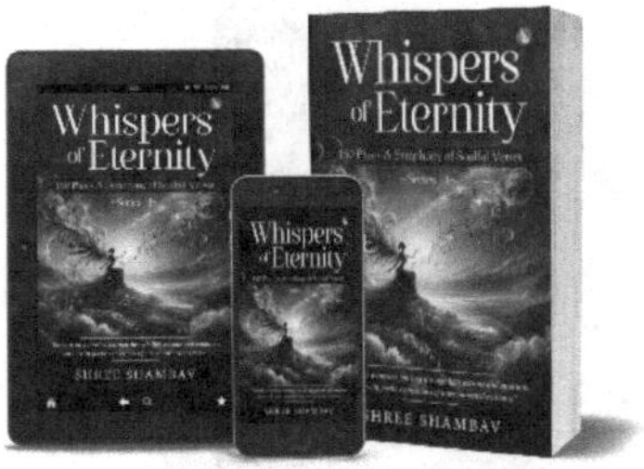

Step into the soul-stirring world of *Whispers of Eternity* by Shree Shambav, a collection of over 150 poems that capture the essence of the human experience. Divided into sections like "Through the Seasons," "Whispers of Hope," and "Threads of Unity," the book journeys through life's phases, emotions, and the universal connections that bind us all. Shree Shambav's verses touch upon nature, love, and spirituality, inspiring readers to find beauty in the everyday. Each poem is a finely crafted reflection, rich with insight and depth. *Whispers of Eternity* invites readers to pause, reflect, and embark on a timeless journey through the landscapes of the heart and soul.

Life Changing Journey Series I and II

In Life Changing Journey - 365 Inspirational Quotes Series I, Shree Shambav curates a powerful collection of 365 original quotes across fourteen chapters, each crafted to touch the heart of our daily lives. More than a simple compilation, this series speaks directly to personal experiences with wisdom and depth. Quotes like, "The most beautiful things are unseen but can be felt," echo the quiet beauty of life's intangible moments. Another, "Giving up is easier; holding oneself up is wiser," provides a guiding light in challenging times. Life Changing Journey reveals the transformative power of carefully chosen words, inspiring readers to find strength and new perspectives on their paths. Through Shree Shambav's work, readers are reminded of the wisdom and resilience hidden within each day.

Twenty + One - 21 Short Stories Series I and II

In *Twenty + One - Short Stories*, Shree Shambav brings to life the often-overlooked characters of nature—trees, animals, and mountains—revealing their intrinsic worth beyond mere utility. With poetic personification, he gives voice to these silent beings, some of whom are lucky enough to have names, titles, and rare human protection. Mountains, usually seen as mere landmarks, are depicted with reverence, emphasising their enduring presence. The stories build a bridge between humans and the natural world, showing that pain, grief, and resilience are shared across all forms of life. Shambav invites readers to empathise with the silent struggles of trees and animals, inspiring a fresh perspective on ecology and our responsibility towards the environment. This collection is a call to honour our connection to nature, encouraging readers to foster compassion and respect for all life.

Learn To Love Yourself

Learn to Love Yourself is a powerful invitation to turn inward in a world focused on external validation and superficial measures. Through ten transformative chapters, each offering a key rule for self-love, readers are guided to uncover their inner beauty, cultivate personal strength, and develop a solid foundation of self-acceptance. This journey goes beyond momentary happiness; it's about building an authentic relationship with yourself that fosters resilience, joy, and fulfilment. From embracing your unique qualities and practising compassion to setting boundaries and pursuing what makes you come alive, this book provides essential insights and practical guidance. Let *Learn to Love Yourself* be your trusted companion on this path, inspiring you to unlock the limitless potential within and find true inner peace.

The Power of Letting Go

The Power of Letting Go invites you to release attachments, fears, and expectations, guiding you toward true inner freedom and joy. With deep insights, practical exercises, and timeless wisdom, this book equips you to face life's challenges with resilience and grace. It explores the essence of attachment, embraces the power of seven-year growth cycles, and teaches the art of forgiveness as a key to a fulfilled life. Each chapter brings concepts to life through relatable analogies and real stories, making profound ideas both accessible and engaging. Let this book serve as your beacon for self-discovery and spiritual awakening, helping you navigate uncertainties and unlock your potential for a joyful, meaningful existence.

A Journey of Lasting Peace

A Journey of Lasting Peace is a transformative guide to self-love, inner peace, and personal strength, where Shree Shambav leads readers through 18 powerful principles for discovering their true selves. Each chapter explores vital themes, from the quest for inner peace and the importance of self-awareness to the healing practices of mindfulness and yoga. Through practical strategies, reflective exercises, and heartfelt stories, this book offers a clear roadmap to a more authentic and fulfilling life.

Whether you seek to embrace imperfection, establish healthy boundaries, or reconnect with nature, A Journey of Lasting Peace provides the wisdom to navigate life's challenges and find enduring tranquillity. Perfect for anyone on a journey of self-discovery, this inspiring work gently reminds us that lasting peace starts within.

Astrology Unveiled: Series I and V

Astrology Unveiled: Foundations of Ancient Wisdom invites you to unlock the mysteries of astrology, offering timeless knowledge rooted in the teachings of ancient sages. This comprehensive guide explores fundamental principles like Rashi, Graha, Bhava, and Divisional charts, making it an essential resource for beginners and intermediate students alike.

With logical explanations and practical applications, Shree Shambav skilfully blends ancient insights with modern understanding. Rich in examples, detailed explanations, and engaging exercises, this book serves as an illuminating path to mastering Vedic astrology.

Embark on a transformative cosmic journey, discovering how astrology can unveil your destiny, guide life's choices, and support your spiritual growth.

The Entitlement Trap: Get Over It, Get On It

Are you feeling stuck in a cycle of blame and dissatisfaction? The Entitlement Trap: Get Over It, Get On It offers a transformative path to reclaiming your personal power. This insightful guide helps you break free from the mindset of victimhood and empowers you to take control of your life. Inside, you'll discover how to redefine success, prioritize your true values, and live with purpose. Through practical strategies, you'll learn to embrace simplicity, connect with nature, and leave a lasting legacy. Get ready to shift from powerless to empowered and create a life you love!

Whispers of a Dying Soul: Unspoken Regrets and Unlived Dreams

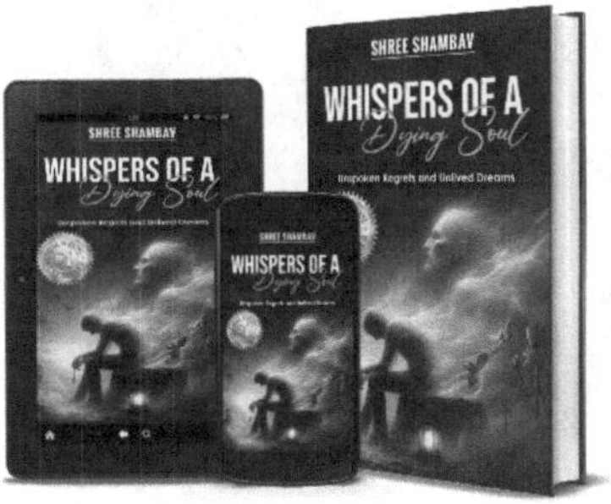

Whispers of a Dying Soul embarks on a profound journey that delves into the silent longings we often carry but seldom express. This powerful exploration uncovers the unspoken emotions that shape our lives—missed opportunities, unfulfilled dreams, and the quest for authenticity. Through heartfelt reflections and transformative insights, this book invites you to confront your regrets and turn them into powerful catalysts for growth and healing.

Whispers of the Soul: A Journey Through Haiku Series I to IV

Whispers of the Soul: A Journey Through Haiku is a poetic invitation to pause and rediscover life's hidden beauty. This transformative collection of haikus explores themes of nature, mindfulness, love, and the human journey, offering profound reflections on universal experiences. Divided into five series, the book delves into nature's elegance, the depths of inner stillness, the tenderness of human connection, the passage of life's seasons, and the mysteries beyond the self. Each haiku captures fleeting moments with timeless grace, guiding readers toward peace, self-discovery, and a renewed appreciation for life's simplest wonders. This is more than poetry—it's a soulful journey.

The Power of Words: Transforming Speech, Transforming Lives

The Power of Words: Transforming Speech, Transforming Lives, illuminates the profound influence of our everyday language. This book explores how words can heal or harm, connect or divide, urging readers to embrace mindful communication. It delves into the "Sins of Speaking," such as gossip and judgment, while celebrating virtues like honesty, kindness, and authenticity. With practical strategies for transformation and a focus on the art of listening, Shree Shambav offers a roadmap to elevate our conversations. Perfect for both personal growth and professional development, this guide inspires readers to use their words to create peace, foster deeper connections, and lead a life of integrity and purpose.

The Art of Intentional Living: Minimalism for a Life of Purpose

In a world that celebrates more, The Art of Intentional Living invites you to embrace less. This powerful guide explores how minimalism can transform every aspect of your life—your space, your time, and your mind—by removing distractions and focusing on what truly matters.

Through simple yet profound principles, you'll learn to:

- Declutter your physical and digital space
- Prioritise what aligns with your values
- Create time for meaningful connections and experiences
- Cultivate a life of purpose, peace, and clarity

Awakening the Infinite: The Power of Consciousness in Transforming Life

In a fragmented world, Awakening the Infinite explores the power of consciousness to heal, transform, and unite. This book takes you on an experiential journey, revealing how awareness shapes reality and connects us to universal wisdom. Through spiritual teachings, introspection, and practical insights, it helps you uncover your soul's true purpose. Transformative practices guide you toward emotional healing, clarity, and personal growth. As you deepen your awareness, you'll forge a profound connection with yourself and the world around you. Embracing this journey leads to a life of mindfulness, authenticity, and purpose. Ultimately, it is an invitation to awaken the infinite potential within.

Beyond the Veil: A Journey Through Life After Death

Discover the Eternal Mystery of Life After Death What happens when we die? Is it the end, or a transition to something greater? In Beyond the Veil: A Journey Through Life After Death, explore humanity's greatest mystery through the lens of science, spirituality, and philosophy.

From near-death experiences to ancient spiritual teachings, this transformative book bridges the gap between the physical and the infinite, offering profound insights into the afterlife. Whether you're seeking comfort, answers, or inspiration, this journey will deepen your understanding of life, death, and what lies beyond.

Bonds Beyond Blood - Where love builds bridges, and bonds defy blood

Roots and Resilience is a poignant tale set against the quiet rhythm of suburban life, where a family grows strong through love, humility, and sacrifice. But when dreams collide with harsh realities and tragedy strikes, their foundation is shaken, and the true test of their bond begins. At the center stands a man, torn between honoring his past and forging a future amidst silent struggles within his marriage and the unspoken weight of grief. As the family navigates heartbreak, healing, and the quiet work of rebuilding, they discover that even broken roots can bloom again. This emotional journey is a testament to the resilience of the human spirit, the redemptive power of forgiveness, and the enduring strength found in choosing love—especially when life is at its most imperfect.

A Journey into Spiritual Maturity - 12 Golden Rules for Inner Transformation

In A Journey into Spiritual Maturity: 12 Golden Rules for Inner Transformation, Shree Shambav offers a soul-stirring path to self-discovery and inner peace. Blending timeless wisdom with practical tools, this book helps you release attachments, embrace change, and live with intention. Through inspiring stories and guided reflection, you'll learn to nurture self-love, deepen your relationships, and find freedom in authenticity.

Each golden rule is a beacon, illuminating the way toward a more meaningful, compassionate life. It is not just a guide—it's a companion for your soul's awakening. Let this journey lead you home to yourself.

9 789334 283471

Printed at Repro India Ltd.